Federal Financial Institutions Examination Council

ANNUAL REPORT 2011

Board of Governors of the Federal Reserve System, Consumer Financial Protection Bureau , Federal Deposit Insurance Corporation, National Credit Union Administration, Office of the Comptroller of the Currency, State Liaison Committee

Federal Financial Institutions Examination Council

ANNUAL REPORT 2011

Board of Governors of the Federal Reserve System, Consumer Financial Protection Bureau, Federal Deposit Insurance Corporation, National Credit Union Administration, Office of the Comptroller of the Currency, State Liaison Committee

MEMBERS OF THE COUNCIL

Debbie Matz, *Chairman*
Chairman
National Credit Union Administration

John Walsh, *Vice Chairman*
Acting Comptroller of the Currency
Office of the Comptroller of the Currency

Daniel K. Tarullo
Member, Board of Governors of the
Federal Reserve System

Martin J. Gruenberg
Acting Chairman
Federal Deposit Insurance Corporation

Richard Cordray
Director
Consumer Financial Protection Bureau

John Munn
Director, Nebraska Department of
Banking & Finance

LETTER OF TRANSMITTAL

Federal Financial Institutions
    Examination Council
Arlington, VA 22226
March 30, 2012

The President of the Senate
The Speaker of the House of Representatives

Pursuant to the provisions of section 1006(f) of the Financial Institutions Regulatory and Interest Rate Control Act of 1978 (12 U.S.C. § 3305), I am pleased to submit the 2011 Annual Report of the Federal Financial Institutions Examination Council.

Respectfully,

Debbie Matz
Chairman

TABLE OF CONTENTS

MESSAGE FROM THE CHAIRMAN

FFIEC Chairman Debbie Matz

I am pleased to report to you as the Chairman of the Federal Financial Institutions Examination Council (FFIEC or Council), the first time in almost 25 years the National Credit Union Administration has chaired the Council.

FFIEC member agencies include the Board of Governors of the Federal Reserve System, the Federal Deposit Insurance Corporation (FDIC), the Office of the Comptroller of the Currency (OCC), the National Credit Union Administration (NCUA) and the State Liaison Committee. In 2011, as a part of the Dodd-Frank Wall Street Reform and Consumer Protection Act of 2010 (Dodd-Frank Act), the Consumer Financial Protection Bureau (CFPB) was added as a member agency to the Council.

In 2011, the Council itself experienced significant changes. In addition to welcoming CFPB as a new agency member, a new acting chairman represented FDIC, and OCC absorbed the Office of Thrift Supervision (OTS). These transitions, particularly the departure of OTS and the installation of CFPB on FFIEC task forces, provided the Council with new perspectives and insights, including a heightened emphasis on financial issues affecting American consumers.

Through the leadership of the Council and the supporting efforts of its task forces, we made substantive efforts to apply and implement certain provisions of the Dodd-Frank Act, the most comprehensive and significant reform legislation affecting the financial sector in a generation. This effort will continue throughout 2012. Notable accomplishments in 2011,

achieved through the work of the FFIEC task forces, subcommittees, and working groups, include the following:

- Renewed emphasis on the work of the FFIEC Appraisal Subcommittee (ASC), which saw its mandate substantially enhanced as a result of the Dodd-Frank Act. At the direction of the Council principals, member agencies committed to designating higher level, senior executive members to serve on the ASC, with the express intention of providing it with a higher level of strategic planning and guidance. With the new structure in place, the ASC is now better positioned to implement several new programs and projects throughout 2012 and beyond: including rulemaking, establishing an advisory committee, and implementing an appraiser hotline as required by the Dodd-Frank Act.

- Issued a Supplement to the 2005 Guidance on Authentication in an Internet Banking Environment to reinforce the necessary risk management framework to mitigate ongoing cyber risk. Updated the Information Technology Examination Handbook to address ongoing risk concerns in the electronic banking area.

- Launched the Nationwide Mortgage Licensing System and Registry for federally regulated institutions in accordance with the Secure and Fair Enforcement for Mortgage Licensing Act of 2008 (the SAFE Act). Released related examination procedures in late 2011.

- Approved an additional senior program administrator position for the Examiner Education Office to continue providing exceptional specialized examiner training.

- Hired a new Executive Secretary, a critical position for the Council and its staff. Managed a seamless transition between the incumbent and the new Executive Secretary.

As we move forward in 2012, FFIEC will continue to emphasize collaborative efforts to jointly draft and issue guidance and other important documents to support the financial safety and soundness of our federally insured institutions as they weather the ongoing financial challenges. FFIEC encourages and facilitates open communication and inclusion among participating agency members.

As Council Chairman, I remain committed to advancing the mission of FFIEC to coordinate regulatory reporting requirements and examination procedures. Our goal is to help our institutions and U.S. consumers achieve financial success in 2012 and beyond.

OVERVIEW OF THE
FEDERAL FINANCIAL INSTITUTIONS
EXAMINATION COUNCIL OPERATIONS

The Federal Financial Institutions Examination Council (FFIEC or Council) was established on March 10, 1979, pursuant to title X of the Financial Institutions Regulatory and Interest Rate Control Act of 1978 (FIRIRCA), Public Law 95-630. The purpose of title X, cited as the Federal Financial Institutions Examination Council Act of 1978, was to create a formal interagency body empowered to prescribe uniform principles, standards, and report forms for the federal examination of financial institutions by the Board of Governors of the Federal Reserve System (FRB), the Federal Deposit Insurance Corporation (FDIC), the National Credit Union Administration (NCUA), and the Office of the Comptroller of the Currency (OCC) and to make recommendations to promote uniformity in the supervision of financial institutions. To encourage the application of uniform examination principles and standards by the state and federal supervisory authorities, the Council established, in accordance with the requirement of the statute, an advisory State Liaison Committee (SLC). In accordance with the Financial Services Regulatory Relief Act of 2006, the Chair of the State Liaison Committee was added as a voting member of the Council in October 2006. In accordance with the Dodd-Frank Wall Street Reform and Consumer Protection Act of 2010, the Director of the Consumer Financial Protection Bureau (CFPB) was added as a voting member of the Council in July 2011, replacing the Director of the former Office of Thrift Supervision (OTS).[1]

The Council is responsible for developing uniform reporting systems for federally supervised financial institutions, their holding companies, and the nonfinancial institution subsidiaries of those institutions and holding companies. It conducts schools for examiners employed by the five federal member agencies represented on the Council and makes those schools available to employees of state agencies that supervise financial institutions.

The Council was given additional statutory responsibilities by section 340 of the Housing and Community Development Act of 1980, Public Law 96-399. Among these responsibilities are the implementation of a system to facilitate public access to data that depository institutions must disclose under the Home Mortgage Disclosure Act of 1975 (HMDA) and the aggregation of annual HMDA data, by census tract, for each metropolitan statistical area.

Title XI of the Financial Institutions Reform, Recovery, and Enforcement Act of 1989 established the Appraisal Subcommittee within the Council. The functions of the subcommittee are (1) monitoring the requirements, including a code of professional responsibility, established by states for the certification and licensing of individuals who are qualified to perform appraisals in connection with federally related transactions; (2) monitoring the appraisal standards established by the federal financial institution regulatory

agencies and the former Resolution Trust Corporation; (3) maintaining a national registry of appraisers who are certified and licensed by a state, and are also eligible to perform appraisals in federally related transactions; and (4) monitoring the practices, procedures, activities, and organizational structure of the Appraisal Foundation, a nonprofit educational corporation established by the appraisal industry in the United States.

The Secure and Fair Enforcement for Mortgage Lending Act of 2008 (SAFE Act), enacted as title V of the Housing and Economic Recovery Act of 2008, established the responsibility for the federal banking agencies, through the FFIEC and in conjunction with the Farm Credit Administration (FCA), to develop and maintain a system for registering employees of depository institutions and certain of their subsidiaries' loan originators with the Nationwide Mortgage Licensing System and Registry (NMLSR). The SAFE Act and implementing regulations require certain information about loan originators to be furnished to the NMLSR information concerning an employee's identity, including: (A) fingerprints for submission to the Federal Bureau of Investigation and any governmental agency or entity authorized to receive such information for a state and national criminal history background check; and (B) personal history and experience, including authorization for the NMLSR to obtain information related to any administrative, civil, or criminal findings by any governmental jurisdiction. The NMLSR began

---

1. The Director of OTS was a voting member of the Council until July 21, 2011, when the functions of the OTS were transferred to the OCC.

accepting registrations on January 31, 2011 and the NMLSR will be fully operational by December 31, 2012. On July 21, 2011, pursuant to the Dodd-Frank Act, the authority for rulemaking and authority to develop and maintain the NMLSR generally transferred to the CFPB.

The Council has six members, and in 2011 it was comprised of a member of the FRB appointed by the Chairman of the Board, the Chairman of the FDIC, the Chairman of the Board of the NCUA, the Comptroller of the Currency, the Director of the OTS (until July 21, 2011), and the Chairman of the SLC. The Director of the CFPB joined the council membership upon his appointment on January 4, 2012.

There are six staff task forces to effectively administer the full spectrum of projects in the Council's functional areas, including but not limited to researching future enhancements for reporting, examiner training products, and examiner guidance. The task forces are each comprised of six senior officials, drawn from the five federal member agencies and a representative of the SLC. Each is tasked

with one of the following subject matters:

- Consumer Compliance

- Examiner Education

- Information Sharing

- Reports

- Supervision

- Surveillance Systems

The Council has a Legal Advisory Group (LAG), composed of the general or chief counsel of each member to provide support to the Council and staff in the substantive areas of concern. The task forces and the LAG provide research and develop analytical papers and proposals on the issues that the Council addresses. In addition, the Council also has an Agency Liaison Group, composed of senior officials responsible for coordinating the FFIEC work of their respective agencies' staff members.

Administration of the Council

The Council holds regular meetings at least twice a year. Other Council meetings may be con-

vened whenever called by the Chairman or four or more Council members. The Council's activities are funded in several ways. Most of the Council's funds are derived from assessments on its five federal member agencies. It receives tuition fees from non-agency attendees to cover some of the costs associated with its examiner education program. The Council also receives reimbursement for the services it provides to support preparation of the quarterly Uniform Bank Performance Report.

In 2011, the FRB continued to provide budget and accounting services to the Council. The Council is supported by a small, full-time administrative staff in its operations office and in its examiner education program, which are located at the FDIC's L. William Seidman Center in Arlington, Virginia. Each Council staff member is detailed (some permanently) from one of the five member agencies represented on the Council.

RECORD OF COUNCIL ACTIVITIES

The Federal Financial Institutions Examination Council in session.

The following section is a chronological record of the official actions taken by the FFIEC during 2011 pursuant to the Federal Financial Institutions Examination Council Act of 1978, as amended, and the Home Mortgage Disclosure Act (HMDA).

February 7, 2011

Action. Approved the issuance of the Council's annual interagency awards.

Explanation. The Council has an interagency awards program that recognizes individuals of the member agencies who have provided outstanding service to the Council on interagency projects and programs during the previous year.

February 7, 2011

Action. Approved the Central Data Repository (CDR) Steering Committee's Task Order #7.

Explanation. The Council is required to approve task orders that exceed a specific dollar amount. Task Order #7 covers funds for CDR enhancements to improve Call Report processing, public data distribution, and Uniform Bank Performance Report processing. Task Order #7 also includes a reallocation of funds within the budget and a setting aside of funds for a bonus payment to the contractor should performance goals be met.

March 8, 2011

Action. Approved the 2010 annual report of the Council to the Congress.

Explanation. The legislation establishing the Council requires that, not later than April 1 of each year, the Council publish an annual report covering its activities during the preceding year.

March 8, 2011

Action. Approved the appointment of six task force chairs.

Explanation. The chairs for all six standing task forces are approved annually and are drawn from management and staff of the five federal member agencies and representatives of the State Liaison Committee (SLC).

Chairman Matz engaged in discussions during the September 2011 Council meeting.

March 8, 2011

Action. Approved re-appointment of At-Large SLC Member, Charles A. Vice, Kentucky Department of Financial Institutions Commissioner.

Explanation. The Council approves two of the five SLC members—those who are not officially designated by the Conference of State Banking Supervisors, the American Council of State Savings Supervisors, or the National Association of State Credit Union Supervisors.

April 11, 2011

Action. Approved the issuance of the Council's annual interagency awards for three additional nominations.

Explanation. The Council has an interagency awards program that recognizes individuals of the member agencies who have pro-

vided outstanding service to the Council on interagency projects and programs during the previous year.

September 2, 2011

Action. Approved the appointment of a new Executive Secretary, Judith E. Dupre.

Explanation. The Executive Secretary role is competitively filled by a candidate from one of the five federal member agencies of the Council.

September 6, 2011

Action. Approved the appointment of a new chair for the Task Force on Examiner Education.

Explanation. The chairs for all six standing task forces are approved annually and are drawn from management and staff of the five federal member agencies and repre-

sentatives of the SLC. The Council also approves any successors to fill an unexpired term of a departing task force chair.

September 30, 2011

Action. Approved a revised HMDA-Required Process Cost Allocation Model for the 2012 Council budget.

Explanation. The Dodd-Frank Act outlines HMDA responsibilities for the newly created Consumer Financial Protection Bureau and removes the Office of Thrift Supervision as a member of the Council. The cost allocation among the five federal member agencies of the Council was adjusted to reflect these changes.

December 9, 2011

Action. Approved the 2012 Council budget.

Explanation. The Council is

required to approve the annual budget that funds the Council's staff, programs, and activities. The Council is also required to approve new staff positions and for the 2012 budget approved the hiring of a fourth Senior Program Administrator. This position is needed due to the significant increases in the training offerings and the number of participants in the Examiner Education program over the past several years.

STATE LIAISON REPORT

State Liaison Committee (from the left to right) David Cotney (MA), Douglas Foster (TX), Chair John Munn (NE), Harold E. Feeney (TX), and Charles A. Vice (KY).

The State Liaison Committee (SLC) consists of five representatives of state regulatory agencies that supervise financial institutions. The representatives are appointed for two-year terms. An SLC member may have his or her two-year term extended by the appointing organization for an additional, consecutive two-year term. Each year, the SLC elects one of its members to serve as chair for 12 months. The Council elects two of the five members. The American Council of State Savings Supervisors, the Conference of State Bank Supervisors (CSBS) and the National Association of State Credit Union Supervisors designate the other three members.

The SLC is represented on the Council's task forces and working groups by state supervisors from around the country. The CSBS provides staff support to the SLC representatives and serves as the primary liaison to the FFIEC staff for all administrative matters.

In response to their role on the Council, the SLC meets in person before each Council meeting to review the agenda and discuss topics of interest which may come before the Council. The members of the SLC are an important conduit to their state colleagues to advocate for the actions of the Council.

ACTIVITIES OF THE INTERAGENCY STAFF TASK FORCES

Task Force on Consumer Compliance

The Task Force on Consumer Compliance promotes policy coordination, a common supervisory approach, and uniform enforcement of consumer protection laws and regulations. The task force identifies and analyzes emerging consumer compliance issues and develops proposed policies and procedures to foster consistency among the agencies. Additionally, the task force reviews legislation, regulations, and policies at the state and federal level that may have a bearing on the compliance responsibilities of the member agencies.

During 2011, the task force used two standing subcommittees to help promote its mission: the Community Reinvestment Act (CRA) Subcommittee and the

Home Mortgage Disclosure Act (HMDA)/CRA Data Collection Subcommittee. The task force also creates ad hoc working groups to handle particular projects and assignments. The task force meets monthly to address and resolve common issues in compliance supervision. While significant issues or recommendations are referred to the Council for action, the Council has delegated to the task force the authority to make certain decisions and recommendations.

Initiatives Addressed in 2011

CRA Subcommittee Activities

The CRA Subcommittee has tracked and made publicly available the 2011 List of Distressed or Underserved Non-Metropolitan Middle-Income Geographies. The

2011 list and lists from previous years can be found on the FFIEC Website, along with information about the data sources used to generate the list of distressed or underserved geographies. The agencies issued the list on June 1, 2011.

The CRA Subcommittee also actively explored policies regarding CRA consideration for Small Dollar Loan (SDL) programs. The subcommittee collaborated on the agencies' approach to small-dollar direct loan programs, partnerships, and other initiatives that help address community credit needs in a responsive and sustainable manner. The subcommittee will continue to engage in an interagency effort to support SDL programs initiated through community organization partnerships and will continue to engage in research on the issue, including an analysis of costs and benefits and determining when SDL programs change consumer behavior.

HMDA/CRA Data Collection Subcommittee Activities

The HMDA and CRA Data Collection Subcommittee benefited from the Data Collection System re-architecture which was completed in 2010. The re-architecture initiative resulted in reduced data reporting and processing costs and enhanced agency access to updated HMDA and CRA data.

To reflect the change in costs and agency responsibilities for HMDA data collection, the subcommittee recommended a simplified cost sharing model for HMDA budgetary responsibilities for 2012. The budget was presented to the Coun-

Task Force on Consumer Compliance meeting.

cil for approval on September 30, 2011.

Regulation Z (Truth in Lending)

The task force approved several sets of examination procedures related to Regulation Z.

On January 13, 2011, the task force voted to adopt Regulation Z Examination Procedures revisions to reflect the rule changes required by the Helping Families Save Their Homes Act and Mortgage Disclosure Improvement Act.

On March 10, 2011, the task force voted to adopt Regulation Z Examination Procedures revisions to reflect rule changes required by changes in the Truth in Lending Act related to loan originator compensation, appraisals, and escrow accounts.

On September 30, 2011, the task force adopted by notational vote two changes to the Regulation Z Examinations Procedures. First, threshold adjustments were made to reflect exemption changes that became effective in June 2011. Second, technical clarifications were added to reflect changes from the Credit Card Accountability Responsibility and Disclosure Act of 2009.

Interagency Questions & Answers Regarding Flood Insurance

In 2009, the FFIEC agencies, along with the FCA, proposed and solicited public comments on additional questions and answers regarding insurable value and force placement issues. During 2010, the task force completed its review of the comments. After approval by the task force and agencies, a notice and request for comment was published in the Federal Register on October 17, 2011. The notice finalized two

new questions and answers, one relating to insurable value and one relating to force placement. The notice also withdrew one question and answer regarding insurable value. The agencies also significantly revised two questions and answers regarding force placement of flood insurance, and proposed to revise a previously finalized question and answer. Comments on these three revised questions and answers were due December 1, 2011.

Model Privacy Notice Examination Procedures

On June 9, 2011, the task force approved Model Privacy Notice Examination Procedures. The procedures address the Gramm-Leach-Bliley Act's provisions regarding the treatment by financial institutions of nonpublic personal information about consumers and the implementing regulations published by the federal banking agencies and NCUA.

SAFE Act Examination Procedures

In July 2010, the federal financial agencies issued final rules to implement the registration of mortgage loan originators employed by banks and credit unions and their subsidiaries as required by the SAFE Act. On October 14, 2011, the task force approved a set of standard examination procedures for compliance with the SAFE Act.

Task Force on Examiner Education

The Task Force on Examiner Education is responsible for overseeing the FFIEC's examiner education program on behalf of the Council. The task force promotes interagency education through timely, cost-efficient, state-of-the-art train-

ing programs for agency examiners and staff. The task force develops programs on its own initiative and in response to requests from the Council, Council task forces, and suggestions brought forth by Examiner Education Office (EEO) staff. Each fall, task force staff prepares a training calendar based on demand from the federal member agencies and state financial institution regulators. The task force staff schedules, delivers, and evaluates training programs throughout the year. In 2011, the number of people who attended task force-sponsored training totaled 3,164 (see the table on page 12 for details of participation by program and agency).

Initiatives Addressed in 2011

The Task Force on Examiner Education has continued to ensure that the FFIEC's educational programs meet the needs of agency personnel, are cost–effective, and are widely available. The task force meets monthly with the EEO staff to discuss emerging topics, to review feedback from each course and conference, and to develop a framework for future courses and conferences. The solid partnership between the task force principals and the EEO staff promotes open and regular communication that continues to result in high-quality, well-received training.

Specific accomplishments during 2011 included 15 sessions of two new courses—(1) Structured Finance and (2) Distressed Commercial Real Estate. These courses have been added to the 2012 training calendar with a combined total of 19 sessions. Also since 1999, the FFIEC has provided training and reference information to examiners and the industry via the FFIEC InfoBase, a browser-based product available through the FFIEC Website. The Task Force on Examiner

Task Force on Examiner Education meeting.

Education approves the development and maintenance of the Info-Base product. The InfoBase content is created and updated by members of the Task Force on Supervision's Information Technology (IT) Subcommittee and the Bank Secrecy Act/Anti-Money Laundering (BSA/AML) Working Group. In 2011, the EEO staff in conjunction with the IT Subcommittee continued to coordinate revisions to the IT Examination Handbook InfoBase. Additionally, the EEO staff in conjunction with the BSA/AML Working Group continued to update the BSA/AML Examination Manual InfoBase.

Facilities

The FFIEC rents office space, classrooms, and lodging facilities at the FDIC's Seidman Center in Arlington, Virginia. This facility offers convenient access to two auditoriums and numerous classrooms.

Course Catalogue and Schedule

The course catalogue and schedule

are available online at www.ffiec. gov/exam/education.htm.

Additionally, a printed copy of the 2012 course catalogue and schedule are available from the EEO. To obtain a copy, contact

Karen K. Smith, Manager
FFIEC Examiner Education Office
3501 Fairfax Drive
Room B-3030
Arlington, VA 22226-3550

Phone: (703) 516-5588

Task Force on Information Sharing

The Task Force on Information Sharing promotes the sharing of electronic information among the FFIEC agencies in support of the supervision, regulation, and deposit insurance responsibilities of financial institution regulators. The task force provides a forum for FFIEC member agencies to discuss and address issues affecting the quality, consistency, efficiency, and security of interagency information sharing. Significant matters are referred, with recommendations, to the Council for action, and the task force has delegated authority from the Council to take certain actions.

To the extent possible, the agencies build on each other's information databases to minimize duplication of effort and promote consistency. The agencies participate in a program to share, in accordance with agency policy, electronic versions of their reports of examination, inspection reports, and other communications with financial institutions. The agencies also provide each other with access to their organizations' structure, as well as

Steve Gulbrandsen instructing financial institution examiners during FFIEC's Commercial Real Estate Analysis course.

financial and supervisory information on their regulated entities. The task force and its working groups use a collaborative website to share information among the FFIEC agencies. The task force maintains a "Data Exchange Summary" listing the data files exchanged among the FFIEC agencies and a repository of communications and documents critical to information sharing.

The task force has established three working groups to address technology development issues, to perform interagency reconciliation of financial institution structure data, and to develop interagency identity management. In addition, the task force receives demonstrations and reports on agency, financial industry, and other FFIEC initiatives pertaining to technology development; including the production and development status of the interagency Central Data Repository.

2011 FFIEC Training by Agency and Sponsored—Actual, as of December 31, 2011

Event Name	FRB	FRB State Sponsored	FDIC	FDIC State Sponsored	NCUA	OCC	OTS	FCA	FHFB	Other	Total
Advanced BSA/AML Conference	22	13	34	7	6	11	6	0	0	6	105
Advanced Cash Flow Concepts & Analysis: Beyond	21	11	57	0	12	26	7	4	1	5	144
Advanced Commercial Credit Analysis	13	8	43	12	11	25	6	3	1	1	123
Anti-Money Laundering Workshop	11	10	44	6	5	0	0	0	0	4	80
Advanced Fraud Investigation Techniques for Examiners	6	9	8	0	8	3	1	1	0	0	36
Asset Management Forum	22	10	44	15	4	8	15	0	0	0	118
Capital Markets Conference	22	20	91	13	20	20	6	4	4	27	227
Capital Markets Specialists Conference	17	3	78	7	8	18	18	19	8	2	178
Cash Flow Construction and Analysis	15	15	55	15	22	46	3	3	0	2	176
Commercial Real Estate	48	19	278	47	33	46	20	2	3	2	498
Community Financial Institutions Lending Forum	18	13	42	5	16	11	3	6	0	1	115
Distressed Commercial Real Estate Analysis	19	7	130	16	8	16	4	0	3	0	203
Financial Crimes Seminar	12	25	83	6	15	9	9	3	1	3	166
Fraud Identification On-line Training	0	0	21	0	3	2	1	0	0	0	27
Information Technology Symposium	0	0	0	0	0	0	0	0	0	0	0
Fundamentals of Fraud	0	0	7	5	9	14	2	1	0	1	39
Information Technology Conference	35	6	41	6	14	52	0	5	4	0	163
Instructor Training School	30	0	0	0	1	1	0	2	0	3	37
International Banking School	1	4	9	0	1	4	1	0	1	1	22
International Banking (Self-study)	6	0	9	0	0	6	0	0	0	1	22
Payments Systems Risk Conference	24	6	21	10	5	24	0	0	1	2	93
Real Estate Appraisal Review School II	15	11	42	0	3	0	0	2	0	3	76
Real Estate Appraisal Review I (On-line)	2	0	45	0	6	0	0	0	0	0	53
Supervisory Updates & Emerging Issues	50	33	151	23	15	39	7	6	9	3	336
Structured Finance: Investment Analysis & Risk Management	21	7	56	0	3	5	4	0	1	0	97
Testifying School	0	0	19	1	1	9	0	0	0	0	30
Grand Total	*430*	*230*	*1,408*	*194*	*229*	*395*	*113*	*61*	*37*	*67*	*3,164*
Percentage	13.59	7.27	44.50	6.13	7.24	12.48	3.57	1.93	1.17	2.12	100
Combined Agency and Sponsored Percentage	20.86	NA	50.63	NA	7.24	12.48	3.57	1.93	1.17	2.12	100

Initiatives Addressed in 2011

Technology Issues

The mission of the task force is to identify and implement technologies to make the sharing of interagency data more efficient and to accommodate changes in agency databases and technologies. The task force's Technology Working Group (TWG) meets monthly to develop technological solutions that enhance data sharing and to coordinate the automated transfer of data files between the FFIEC agencies. The group tracks weekly developments to provide timely resolutions of data exchange issues.

The TWG continues to develop necessary links and processes to exchange electronic documents, develop an inventory of future technology projects, and upload information to the collaborative website where documents and critical materials pertaining to interagency information exchanges are stored. TWG efforts addressed in 2011 include:

- *Shared National Credit (SNC) Modernization*—Agencies implemented additional SNC schemas as the application provided more functionality.

- *National Information Center (NIC) 2.0*—Agencies implemented two releases in April and December resulting in NIC 2.0 becoming the system of record.

- *Office of Thrift Supervision Dissolution*—Agencies updated their systems to address transitioning of supervisory authority over state chartered thrifts to the FDIC, federally chartered thrifts to the OCC and savings and loan holding companies to the FRB.

Structure Data Reconciliation

The task force's Structure Data

Task Force on Information Sharing meeting.

Reconciliation Working Group (SDRWG) continued to reconcile structure data about financial institutions regulated by FFIEC agencies to ensure that the information the agencies report is consistent and accurate. The SDRWG's quarterly reconcilements have greatly resolved structure data discrepancies among the agencies. In 2011, the group focused on the reconciliation during the change of supervisory authority from the OTS for state chartered thrifts to the FDIC and federally chartered thrifts to the OCC.

Identity Management

The Identity Management Working Group continued with its efforts to begin developing an Identity Management technology framework within the FFIEC agencies. These continuing efforts are based on a 2010 white paper developed and presented to the agencies' Chief Information Officers. This document discussed the new information challenges presented by the recent financial reforms, and sought a consensus on the scope and urgency of the

efforts needed to meet these challenges going forward.

Task Force on Reports

The law establishing the Council and defining its functions requires the Council to develop uniform reporting systems for federally supervised financial institutions and their holding companies and subsidiaries. To meet this objective, the Council established the Task Force on Reports. The task force helps to develop interagency uniformity in the reporting of periodic information that is needed for effective supervision and other public policy purposes. As a consequence, the task force is concerned with issues such as the development and interpretation of reporting instructions—including responding to inquiries about the instructions from reporting institutions and the public, the application of accounting standards to specific transactions, the development and application of processing standards, the monitoring of data quality, and the assessment of reporting burden. In addition, the task force works with other organizations, including the Securities and Exchange Commission, the Financial Accounting Standards Board (FASB), and the American Institute of Certified Public Accountants. The task force is also responsible for any special projects related to these subjects that the Council may assign.

To help the task force carry out its responsibilities, working groups are organized as needed to handle specialized or technical accounting, reporting, instructional, and processing matters. In this regard, the task force has established a Central Data Repository (CDR) Steering Committee to make business decisions needed to ensure the continued success of the CDR system, monitor its ongoing performance, and report on its status. The CDR is a secure shared database for collecting, managing, validating, and distributing data reported in the quarterly Consolidated Reports of Condition and Income (Call Report) filed by insured banks and, beginning in 2012, savings associations. The CDR also processes and distributes the Uniform Bank Performance Report (UBPR) under the oversight of the Task Force on Surveillance Systems.

Task Force on Reports meeting.

Initiatives Addressed in 2011

Reporting Requirements for the Consolidated Reports of Condition and Income

The task force conducted monthly interagency conference calls during 2011 to discuss Call Report instructional matters and related accounting issues to reach uniform interagency positions on these issues.

March 2011 Call Report Revisions

After receiving approval under the Paperwork Reduction Act

(PRA) from the U.S. Office of Management and Budget (OMB), the FDIC, the FRB, and the OCC (collectively, the banking agencies) implemented several revisions to the Call Report in March 2011. The revisions, which had initially been issued for public comment in September 2010, were made to assist the banking agencies and state supervisors in gaining a better understanding of banks' credit and liquidity risk exposures. The reporting changes included additional data on troubled debt restructurings, commercial mortgage-backed securities, deposits maturing within one year, loans and other real estate covered by FDIC loss-sharing agreements, bank-owned life insurance, and trust department collective investment funds; new data on auto loans, deposits obtained through deposit listing services, and assets and liabilities of consolidated variable interest entities and captive insurance subsidiaries; and instructional

revisions relating to construction loans. The Office of Thrift Supervision (OTS) implemented several of the same reporting changes in the Thrift Financial Report (TFR) filed by savings associations.

TFR-to-Call Report Conversion

After careful review, the banking agencies and the OTS (collectively, the agencies) concluded in late 2010 that having common financial reports and reporting processes among all FDIC-insured banks and savings institutions would be more efficient than maintaining the TFR as a separate report solely for savings associations after the abolition of the OTS and the transfer of its functions to the banking agencies on July 21, 2011. Common reporting also would lead to more uniform comparisons of financial condition, performance, and trends among institutions. For these reasons, the agencies agreed to propose requiring savings associations to begin filing the Call

Report in place of the TFR effective March 31, 2012. Following task force approval, the agencies jointly published an initial PRA Federal Register notice in February 2011 requesting comment on the proposed migration of savings associations from the TFR to the Call Report. After considering the eight comments received on the proposal, the agencies agreed to proceed with the TFR-to-Call Report conversion for savings associations in March 2012, but to allow individual institutions to elect to begin filing the Call Report in either September or December 2011. Following task force approval, the agencies jointly published a final PRA Federal Register notice on this conversion in July 2011. The final notice also addressed the elimination of the TFR's interest rate risk schedule and the OTS Interest Rate Risk Model after the filing of the year-end 2011 TFR. OMB approved this reporting change for savings associations in August 2011. The OTS issued a CEO Letter in July 2011 to notify savings associations about their migration to the Call Report and the agencies have since conducted or participated in various outreach activities to assist savings associations in preparing to file Call Reports.

2012 Call Report Revisions

In the second quarter of 2011, the task force began evaluating several recommendations from the banking agencies for potential Call Report revisions to be implemented in 2012. As the task force considered the purposes for which the banking agencies and state supervisors would use the recommended new data and the need for certain proposed instructional revisions, it also sought to limit the reporting changes that would apply to institutions with less than $1 billion in total assets. In the fourth quarter, the task

force approved the inclusion of a number of reporting and instructional revisions in a proposal to be issued for comment. The proposed new data items, which are focused primarily on larger institutions, would help the banking agencies and state supervisors better understand these institutions' lending activities and credit-risk exposures by providing information on selected loan origination activity, the composition of the loan loss allowance, mortgage loan representation and warranty reserves, and past due and nonaccrual purchased credit-impaired loans. These proposed revisions would take effect in June 2012. Two other proposed changes would be made in March 2012 in connection with the initial filing of the Call Report by savings associations: new items for reporting on Qualified Thrift Lender compliance and revisions to certain items used to calculate the leverage ratio denominator. In November 2011, the banking agencies published an initial PRA Federal Register notice requesting comment for 60 days on the proposed 2012 Call Report revisions. The comment period closed in January 2012 and the task force will review and consider the comments received to determine how to finalize the proposal.

Assessment-Related Reporting Changes

The FDIC adopted a final rule in February 2011 that redefined the deposit insurance assessment base for all insured depository institutions as required by the Dodd-Frank Act. The final rule, which took effect in the second quarter of 2011, also revised the risk-based assessment system for large institutions, generally those with at least $10 billion in total assets. In coordination with the staff in the FDIC's Division of Insurance and Research (DIR), the task force

approved an initial PRA Federal Register notice soliciting comment for 60 days on proposed reporting changes to the Call Report, the TFR, and the Report of Assets and Liabilities of U.S. Branches and Agencies of Foreign Banks (FFIEC 002 report) that would provide the information needed to implement the redefined assessment base and the revised large institution assessment system beginning with the second quarter 2011 reports. The notice was published in March 2011. Because of unanticipated comments from large institutions about the subprime and leveraged loan definitions in the revised assessment system for such institutions and the challenges in operationalizing their reporting under the new definitions, a transitional approach was developed for reporting these loans until October 1, 2011. The agencies then requested and received emergency clearance under the PRA from OMB in June 2011 rather than continuing the normal clearance process for the assessment-related reporting changes. The use of emergency clearance procedures was intended to provide certainty to institutions on a timely basis concerning the initial collection of the new assessment data as of the June 30, 2011, report date as called for under the FDIC's final rule.

Upon OMB's emergency approval of the assessment-related reporting changes, which extended only through the December 31, 2011, report date, the task force began the normal PRA clearance process anew. Following task force approval, the banking agencies and the OTS jointly published a second initial PRA Federal Register notice for these reporting changes for a 60-day comment period in July 2011. In response to large institutions' continued concerns about the subprime and leveraged loan definitions used for assessment purposes, the FDIC's DIR staff agreed to review these definitions and consider changes that would be consistent with the FDIC's goals of better differentiating among those institutions for risk and taking a more forward looking view of risk. Any such changes would require rulemaking by the FDIC. The banking agencies also extended the transitional approach to reporting subprime and leveraged loans until April 1, 2012. Based on input provided by the DIR staff concerning the comments received on the second initial PRA notice, the task force completed and approved the final PRA Federal Register notice for the assessment-related reporting changes, which the agencies published in December 2011. No comments were received on the final PRA notice, for which the comment period closed in January 2012. OMB approval of the assessment-related reporting changes under normal PRA clearance procedures is pending.

FASB's Accounting Standards Codification

In March 2011, the task force completed the incorporation of references to the FASB's Accounting Standards Codification into the Call Report instruction book while retaining references to the often more familiar pre-Codification standards. The FASB established the Codification as the single source of authoritative nongovernmental U.S. generally accepted accounting principles in June 2009, replacing the former standards-based model with a topically-based model. The FFIEC's instruction book update for September 2010 included a revised glossary section of the book that added Codification references throughout the section's entries.

Central Data Repository

During 2011, the banking agencies continued to devote significant staff resources to enhance the CDR for the processing of the quarterly Call Report, production of the UBPR, and the public data distribution (PDD) of those data.

In September 2011, the banking agencies implemented a major CDR enhancement release. The September release included enhancements to improve the PDD, UBPR processing, and the FRB's National Information Center import functionality that is used to manage the CDR structure data. Also included in the release were changes to the CDR system necessary to accommodate the transition of savings associations from the TFR to the Call Report effective March 31, 2012. The system was prepared for and has successfully accepted those filings from saving associations that chose to transition to the Call Report early. That option was open to respondents beginning in September 2011.

Other Activities

In March 2011, OMB approved several changes to the FFIEC 002 report that the FRB had first published for comment on behalf of the banking agencies in August 2010. The revisions, which took effect in March 2011, incorporated several recent bank Call Report revisions into the FFIEC 002 report: additional detail on trading assets, changes to the reporting of certain time deposits, and additional detail and modified criteria for reporting on assets and liabilities measured at fair value.

After receiving OMB approval under the PRA in March 2011, the agencies implemented a limited number of revisions to the

Advanced Capital Adequacy Framework Regulatory Reporting Requirements (FFIEC 101 report). These changes to the report merged the separate banking organization and savings association schedules for calculating total capital, segregated the reporting by bank holding companies of certain restricted core capital elements from other core capital elements, and streamlined the reporting of equity exposures. Following task force approvals, the agencies jointly published initial and final PRA Federal Register notices requesting comment on the proposed reporting changes in October 2010 and January 2011, respectively.

In November 2011, the task force approved, and the FRB published on behalf of the banking agencies, an initial PRA Federal Register notice requesting comment on proposed revisions to the FFIEC 002 report that would take effect in June 2012. These revisions would provide additional detail on trading assets and add a new schedule on loan origination activity similar to the schedule proposed for the Call Report. After the proposal's 60-day comment period closes in January 2012, the task force will consider the comments received and determine how to proceed with the proposed reporting changes.

Task Force on Supervision

The Task Force on Supervision coordinates and oversees matters relating to safety-and-soundness supervision and examination of depository institutions. It provides a forum for Council members to promote quality, consistency, and effectiveness in examination and supervisory practices. While significant issues are referred, with recommendations, to the Council for action, the Council has delegated to the task force the authority to make certain decisions and recommendations, provided all task force members agree. Meetings are held regularly to address and resolve common supervisory issues. The task force has also established and maintains supervisory communication protocols to be used in emergencies. These protocols are periodically tested through table-top exercises with task force members and key supervisory personnel.

The task force has one subcommittee and one permanent working group:

- *The Information Technology (IT) Subcommittee* serves as a forum to address information systems and technology policy issues as they relate to financial institutions and their technology service providers (TSPs). The IT Subcommittee develops and maintains the FFIEC Information Technology Examination Handbook, which consists of a series of topical booklets addressing issues such as information security. The IT Subcommittee also oversees and administers the FFIEC member agencies' Multi-Regional Data Processing Servicer (MDPS) examination and Shared Application Software Review (SASR) programs. Through the FFIEC's MDPS program, the agencies conduct joint IT examinations of the largest and most complex TSPs and other entities that provide critical data processing and related banking services to regulated financial institutions. The SASR program provides a mechanism for the agencies to review and share information on mission-critical software applications, such as loans, deposits, credit, BSA/AML, general ledger sys-

Task Force on Supervision meeting.

tems, and other critical software tools that are used by financial institutions. These programs help the agencies identify potential systemic risks and provide examiners with information that can reduce time and resources needed to examine the IT-related processing operations, software, and outsourced services at user financial institutions. In conjunction with the Task Force on Education, the IT Subcommittee sponsors an annual conference for the agencies' examination staff.

- *The Bank Secrecy Act/Anti-Money Laundering (BSA/AML) Working Group* seeks to enhance coordination of BSA/AML training, guidance, and policy. The coordination includes continuing communication between federal and state banking agencies and the Financial Crimes Enforcement Network. The BSA/AML Working Group also meets periodically with other federal agencies including: the Internal Revenue Service, Securities and Exchange Commission, United States Commodity Futures Trading Commission, Treasury Department's Office of Terrorist Financing and Financial Crimes, and the Office of Foreign Assets Control. The BSA/AML Working Group builds on existing efforts and works to strengthen the activities that are already being pursued by other formal and informal interagency groups providing oversight of various BSA/AML matters. BSA/AML training, guidance, and policy includes: (1) procedures and resource materials for examination purposes; (2) joint examiner training related to the FFIEC's BSA/AML Examination Manual; (3) outreach to the banking industry on BSA/AML policy matters; and (4) other issues related to consistency of BSA/AML supervision.

The task force also establishes ad hoc working groups to handle individual projects and assignments, as needed.

Initiatives Addressed in 2011 *SAFE Act*

A task force working group, together with the Farm Credit Administration (FCA), continued to coordinate efforts among the FFIEC agencies to implement provisions of the Secure and Fair Enforcement for Mortgage Licensing Act of 2008 (the SAFE Act).

The working group's major initiative in 2011 was the successful launch of the Nationwide Mortgage Licensing System and Registry (NMLSR) for federally regulated institutions. As required by the SAFE Act, mortgage loan originators (MLOs) employed by institutions that are regulated by a federal banking agency or the FCA must register with the NMLSR, obtain a unique identifier, and maintain their registration. As envisioned, the NMLSR will improve the flow of information to and between regulators, providing increased accountability and tracking of MLOs, enhancing consumer protections, and providing consumer access to certain information on MLOs.

On January 31, 2011, the FFIEC agencies and FCA announced the opening of the initial registration period for federal registration in the NMLSR. Following the 180-day registration period, which ended on July 29, 2011, any employee of a federally regulated institution who is subject to the registration requirements will be prohibited from originating residential mortgage loans without first meeting such requirements. During the initial registration period 10,507 institutions registered with the NMLSR and 349,791 MLOs completed their registrations. Throughout the initial registration period, the working group monitored the progress of registrations and collaborated to address

questions regarding implementation of their regulations.

On July 21, 2011, pursuant to the Dodd-Frank Act, the CFPB assumed responsibility for developing and maintaining the federal registration system (including rulemaking authority) and supervisory and enforcement authority for SAFE Act compliance for institutions under the CFPB's jurisdiction. On December 19, 2011, the CFPB published an interim final rule establishing a new Regulation G (SAFE Mortgage Licensing Act–Federal Registration of Mortgage Loan Originators). The interim final rule was effective on December 30, 2011 with public comments due February 17, 2012.

Review of Examination Practices

The task force formed a working group to identify opportunities for the agencies to enhance their respective examination practices relative to lessons learned from the recent financial crisis and its aftermath. Within the working group, the FFIEC member agencies shared information on findings related to supervisory matters highlighted by the crisis. Through this information exchange, the agencies independently addressed revisions to their respective examination practices.

Information Technology

Financial institutions' significant use of information technology services, whether generated internally or obtained from third-party service providers, contributes to their operational risk environment in general and their data security risk in particular. A major effort of the IT Subcommittee and agencies is maintaining the FFIEC Information Technology Examination Handbook and providing guidance to the industry on emerging IT issues and risks.

On June 28, 2011, the FFIEC issued a supplement to guidance entitled Authentication in an Internet Banking Environment, issued in 2005 (2005 Guidance). The 2005 Guidance provided a risk-management framework for financial institutions offering Internet-based products and services to their customers. In the Supplement to Authentication in an Internet Banking Environment, the FFIEC member agencies reinforce the risk management framework in the 2005 Guidance and update the agencies' expectations regarding customer authentication, layered security, or other controls in the increasingly hostile online environment.

The IT Subcommittee also facilitated the development and implementation of a new process that member agencies will use to standardize the collection of data from TSPs on regulated financial institutions with which the TSPs have entered into contractual obligations. This process will increase the accuracy of the data needed for supervisory purposes as well as reduce the level of effort and burden on TSPs and the FFIEC member agencies' examiners.

The IT Subcommittee, in conjunction with the Task Force on Examiner Education, sponsors an annual Information Technology conference for the agencies' examination staff on emerging risks and industry best practices. The IT Subcommittee is also responsible for the coordination of the Multi-Regional Data Processing Servicer (MDPS) program oversight, which is ongoing. The FFIEC member agencies examine MDPS organizations because these entities pose a systemic risk to the banking system should one or more have operational or financial problems or fail. Since these companies service banks, thrifts, and credit unions, the FFIEC member agencies conduct interagency examinations of these large TSPs. Interagency examinations provide a single examination report for the service providers. During the year, the IT Subcommittee devoted resources to work streams resulting from the 2011 strategy session with interagency examination teams from each MDPS, including efforts to address supervisory expectations for emerging technologies, products, and services such as managed secured services.

BSA/AML Working Group

The BSA/AML Working Group is responsible for maintaining and providing timely updates to the BSA/AML Examination Manual (Manual) and examination procedures. The agencies' most recent release of updates to the Manual occurred in 2010. A Spanish language translation was coordinated by several of the FFIEC member agencies and posted to the FFIEC Website in 2011.

The BSA/AML working group sponsored its fifth FFIEC Advanced BSA/AML Specialists Conference in July 2011. Feedback from the conference was positive. The agencies continued to share information with the Financial Crimes Enforcement Network and with the Office of Foreign Assets Control.

Task Force on Surveillance Systems

The Task Force on Surveillance Systems oversees the development and implementation of uniform interagency surveillance and monitoring systems. It provides a forum for the member agencies to discuss best practices to be used in those systems and to consider the development of new financial analysis tools. The task force's principal objective has been

to develop and produce the Uniform Bank Performance Report (UBPR). UBPRs present financial data and peer group statistics of individual financial institutions for current and historical periods. These reports are important tools for completing supervisory evaluations of a financial institution's condition and performance, as well as for planning onsite examinations. The banking agencies also use the data from these reports in their automated monitoring systems to identify potential or emerging problems in insured banks.

A UBPR is produced for each commercial bank and insured savings bank in the United States that is supervised by the FRB, the FDIC, or the OCC. UBPR data are also available to all state bank supervisors. While the UBPR is principally designed to meet the examination and surveillance needs of the federal and state banking agencies, the task force also makes the UBPR available to banks and the public through a public website, www.ffiec.gov/UBPR.htm.

Initiatives Addressed in 2011

Improved UBPR Analysis of Deposits

Ratios that analyze core deposits, non-core liabilities, and short-term non-core liabilities were revised to utilize new detail reported beginning with the March 31, 2011 Call Report Schedule RC-E. The revised ratios reflect the increase in the FDIC deposit insurance limit, from $100,000 to $250,000. Ratios found on the UBPR Page 1 Summary Ratios, UBPR Page 4 Balance Sheet $, UBPR Page 6 Balance Sheet %, and UBPR Page 10 Liquidity and Investment Portfolio were affected.

Improved UBPR Analysis of Loans

Ratios that analyze past due and

nonaccrual loans were revised to utilize new detail reported beginning with the March 31, 2001 Call Report Schedules RC-C and RC-N. The Call Report added data on automobile loans and expanded reporting of loans that are troubled debt restructurings by loan category. The task force also implemented new ratios to analyze the impact of government guarantees on past due loans. Ratios found on the UBPR Page 1 Summary Ratios; UBPR Page 7 and Page 7A Analysis of Credit Allowance and Loan Mix; UBPR Page 7B Analysis of Concentrations of Credit; and UPBR Page 8 and Page 8A Analysis of Past Due, Nonaccrual & Restructured Loans & Leases were affected.

Thrift Financial Report Consolidation into Call Report

The Dodd-Frank Act dissolved the OTS, and mandated that thrift institutions formerly regulated by the OTS begin filing Call Reports no later than March 31, 2012. The task force determined that all thrift institutions will be placed into the existing FDIC-insured savings bank peer groups. There are currently four FDIC-insured savings bank peer groups: insured savings banks having assets less than $100 million, insured savings banks having assets between $100 million and $300 million, insured savings banks having assets between $300 million and $1 billion, and insured savings banks having assets greater than $1 billion. The task force further agreed to create a supplementary peer group for mutually owned thrift institutions, using asset size groups that correspond to the current four FDIC-insured savings bank peer groups. The task force is currently taking efforts to ensure that thrift institutions are placed in the existing FDIC-insured savings bank and mutual savings bank peer groups

Task Force on Surveillance Systems meeting.

with the publication of the March 31, 2012 UBPR.

Enhancements to Liquidity and Funding Ratios

In 2010, the task force approved a working group to review UBPR treatment of liquidity measures and overall funding analysis. The working group has concluded its review and has agreed on which ratios should be modified, added, or deleted. The task force has approved the working group's recommendations. The enhancements to the UBPR liquidity and funding ratios are scheduled to be completed in 2012.

Enhancements to Fiduciary Activities Ratios

In 2010, the task force approved a working group to review UBPR treatment of fiduciary data obtained from Call Report Schedule RC-T. The working group has concluded its review and has agreed on which ratios should be modified, added, or deleted. The task force has approved the working group's recommendations. The enhancements to UBPR fiduciary activities data and ratios are scheduled to be completed in 2012.

Enhancements to UBPR Ratio Documentation

The task force is undertaking a complete rewrite of the UBPR User's Guide, which will be refocused as a technical reference manual. In 2011, the task force explored different options of presenting technical data to explain UBPR ratios. The task force agreed to develop an online UBPR technical reference manual as well as an electronic version as a Portable Document Format file. The enhancements to UBPR ratio documentation are scheduled to be completed in 2012.

UBPR Delivered to a Wide Audience

UBPR for December 31, 2010; March 31, 2011; June 30, 2011; and September 30, 2011 were produced and delivered during 2011 to federal and state banking agencies. Additionally, the UBPR website delivered the same data to bankers and the general public. The task force strives to deliver the most up-to-date UBPR data to all users through nightly updates of current and historic UBPR data. Frequent updating allows the UBPR to remain synchronized with new Call Report data as submissions are made by financial institutions.

Projects Planned for 2012

- *Liquidity and funding* — The task force has approved the changes to the existing liquidity and funding UBPR page that were proposed by the working group. These changes provide additional ratios that should enhance liquidity and funding analysis. Changes to the existing liquidity and funding UBPR page are scheduled to be implemented in 2012.

- *Fiduciary activities* — The task force has approved the changes to the existing fiduciary activities UBPR page that were proposed by the working group. This will be the first comprehensive update of information obtained from Call Report Schedule RC-T since the initial 2002 implementation of the fiduciary activities pages. Changes to the existing fiduciary activities pages are scheduled to be implemented in 2012.

- *Improved documentation* — The task force is re-focusing of the existing UBPR User's Guide into a technical reference manual. The new UBPR Users Guide will provide Call Report-based explanations of UBPR ratio calculations. The improved user guide is scheduled to be implemented in 2012.

Information Available on the UBPR Website

UBPR Availability

To provide broad banking industry

and public access to information about the financial condition of insured financial institutions, the task force publishes UBPR data for each institution shortly after the underlying Call Report is filed in the CDR. The UBPR is frequently refreshed to reflect amendments to underlying Call Report data and to incorporate any content-based changes agreed to by the task force. The online UBPR is a dynamic report that is closely synchronized with the underlying Call Report.

Other UBPR Reports

Several web-based statistical reports supporting UBPR analysis are also available and are updated nightly on the website. These reports (1) summarize the performance of all UBPR peer groups (determined by size, location, and business line); (2) detail the distribution of UBPR performance ratios for financial institutions in each of these peer groups; (3) list the individual financial institutions included in each peer group; and (4) compare a financial institutions to the performance of a user-defined custom peer group.

Custom Peer Group Tool

The Custom Peer Group Tool allows bankers, bank supervisors, and the general public to create custom peer groups based on financial and geographical criteria. The tool can then display all UBPR pages with peer group statistics and percentile rankings derived from the custom peer group. The Custom Peer Group Tool can re-compute the entire UBPR using a custom peer group of up to 2,000 banks and deliver the results usually within seconds.

Bulk Data Download

The UBPR database within the CDR, which contains all data appearing on report pages for all financial institutions who file a Call Report, may be downloaded as either a delimited file or in XBRL format. There is no charge for this service and downloads are typically fast.

Please visit www.ffiec.gov/UBPR. htm for additional information about the UBPR, including status, descriptions of pending changes, and the UBPR Users Guide. The site also provides access to the reports described above. For questions about the UBPR contact support by calling 1-888-237-3111, emailing cdr.help@ffiec.gov, or writing the Council at

Federal Financial Institutions Examination Council
Attention: UBPR Coordinator
3501 Fairfax Drive, Room B7081a
Arlington, VA 22226-3550

The Federal Financial Institution Regulatory Agencies and Their Supervised Institutions

The FDIC, OCC, and NCUA have primary federal supervisory jurisdiction over 14,664 domestically chartered banks, thrift institutions, and federally insured credit unions. On December 31, 2011, these financial institutions held total assets of just under $17 trillion. The FRB has primary federal supervisory responsibility for commercial bank holding companies and, as of July 21, 2011, for savings and loan holding companies.

Three banking agencies on the Council have authority to oversee the operations of U.S. branches and agencies of foreign banks. The International Banking Act of 1978 (IBA) authorizes the OCC to license federal branches and agencies of foreign banks and permits U.S. branches that accept only wholesale deposits to apply for insurance with the FDIC. According to the Federal Deposit Insurance Corporation Improvement Act of 1991 (FDICIA), foreign banks that wish to operate insured entities in the United States and accept retail deposits must organize under separate U.S. charters. Existing insured retail branches may continue to operate as branches. The IBA also subjects those U.S. offices of foreign banks to many provisions of the Federal Reserve Act and the Bank Holding Company Act. The IBA gives primary examining authority to the OCC, the FDIC, and various state authorities for the offices within their jurisdictions. The IBA also gives the FRB residual examining authority over all U.S. banking operations of foreign banks. The Dodd-Frank Act provides statutory authority to the CFPB to conduct examinations of insured depository entities with total assets over $10 billion and their affiliates (in addition to certain nonbank entities) to ensure consumer financial products and services conform to Federal consumer financial laws.

Board of Governors of the Federal Reserve System

The Federal Reserve Board (FRB) was established in 1913. It is headed by a seven-member Board of Governors; each member is appointed by the President, with the advice and consent of the Senate, for a 14-year term. Subject to confirmation by the Senate, the President selects one Board member to serve a four-year term as Chairperson and two members to serve as Vice Chairs; one serves in the absence of the Chairperson and the other is designated as Vice Chair for Supervision. One member of the Board of Governors serves as the Board's representative to the FFIEC. The FRB's activities most relevant to the work of the Council are the following:

- overseeing the quality and efficiency of the examination and supervision function of the 12 Federal Reserve Banks;

- monitoring the financial condition, operations, and systemic risk of state member banks (i.e., state-chartered banks that are members of the Federal Reserve System), bank holding companies (BHCs), including financial holding companies (FHCs)[1] and Edge Act and agreement corporations;

- supervising and regulating, in conjunction with the respon-

sible licensing authorities, the international operations of banking organizations headquartered in the United States and the domestic activities of foreign banking organizations;

- developing, issuing, implementing, and communicating regulations, supervisory policies and guidance, and taking appropriate enforcement actions applicable to those organizations that are within the FRB's supervisory oversight authority; and

- approving or denying applications for mergers, acquisitions, and changes in control by state member banks and BHCs (including FHCs), applications for foreign operations of member banks and Edge Act and agreement corporations, and applications by foreign banks to establish or acquire U.S. banks and to establish U.S. branches, agencies, or representative offices.

Other supervisory and regulatory responsibilities of the FRB include monitoring compliance by entities under the Board's jurisdiction with other statutes (e.g., the money-laundering provisions of the Bank Secrecy Act), monitoring compliance with certain statutes that protect consumers in credit and deposit transactions, regulating margin requirements on securities transactions, and regulating transactions between banking affiliates.

Policy decisions are implemented by the FRB or under delegated authority to the Director for the Division of Banking Supervision and Regulation, the Director for the Division of Consumer and Community Affairs, and to the twelve Federal Reserve Banks— each of which has operational responsibility within a specific geographical area. The Reserve

---

1. The FRB's role as the supervisor of a BHC or FHC is to review and assess the consolidated organization's operations, risk-management systems, and capital adequacy to ensure that the holding company and its non-bank subsidiaries do not threaten the viability of the company's depository institutions. In this role, the FRB serves as the "umbrella supervisor" of the consolidated organization. In fulfilling this role, the FRB relies to the fullest extent possible on information and analysis provided by the appropriate supervisory authority of the company's bank, securities, or insurance subsidiaries.

Bank Districts are headquartered in Boston, New York, Philadelphia, Cleveland, Richmond, Atlanta, Chicago, St. Louis, Minneapolis, Kansas City, Dallas, and San Francisco. Each Reserve Bank has a president (chief executive officer) who serves for 5 years and is appointed by the Reserve Bank's class B and class C directors, and other executive officers who report directly to the president. Among other responsibilities, a Reserve Bank employs a staff of examiners who examine state member banks and Edge Act and agreement corporations, conduct BHC inspections, and examine the international operations of foreign banks—whose head offices are usually located within the Reserve Bank's District. When appropriate, examiners also visit the overseas offices of U.S. banking organizations to obtain financial and operating information to evaluate adherence to safe and sound banking practices.

National banks, which must be members of the Federal Reserve System, are chartered, regulated, and supervised by the Office of the Comptroller of the Currency. State-chartered banks may apply to and be accepted for membership in the Federal Reserve System, after which they are subject to the supervision and regulation of the FRB, which is coordinated with the state's banking authority. Insured state-chartered banks

that are not members of the Federal Reserve System are regulated and supervised by the FDIC. The FRB also has overall responsibility for foreign banking operations, including both U.S. banks operating abroad and foreign banks operating branches within the United States.

On July 21, 2010, the President signed the financial regulatory reform bill (the Dodd-Frank Act). The Dodd-Frank Act gives the FRB new responsibilities including:

1. Membership in the newly formed Financial Stability Oversight Council (FSOC). The FSOC's responsibilities include identifying risks to financial stability and promoting market discipline. The FSOC has 10 designated voting members and five designated nonvoting advisory members. The Secretary of Treasury serves as the Chairperson of the FSOC.

2. Supervision of nonbank financial firms that are designated as systemically important by the FSOC.

3. Supervision and regulation of savings and loan holding companies (SLHCs).

4. Development of enhanced prudential standards for large BHCs with $50 billion or more in assets, and for systemically significant FSOC-designated nonbank financial firms (includ-

ing requirements related to capital, liquidity, stress tests, risk management, concentration limits, and credit exposure reporting).

5. Promulgation of risk-management standards and performing an enhanced supervisory role for financial market utilities and payment, clearing, and settlement activities that are designated as systemically important by the FSOC.

Additionally, the Dodd-Frank Act created an independent CFPB, within the Federal Reserve System, and charged it with writing regulations to implement enumerated consumer financial protection laws and supervising financial institutions with assets greater than $10 billion, and their affiliates, for compliance with those laws.

The FRB covers the expenses of its operations with revenue it generates principally from assessments on the 12 Federal Reserve Banks. The Dodd-Frank Act directs the FRB to collect assessments, fees, and other charges that are equal to the expenses incurred by the Federal Reserve to carry out its responsibilities with respect to supervision of (1) BHCs and SLHCs with assets equal to or greater than $50 billion; and (2) all non-bank financial companies supervised by the FRB.

Consumer Financial
Protection Bureau

Consumer Financial Protection Bureau

The Consumer Financial Protection Bureau (CFPB) was created in 2010 by the Dodd-Frank Act, and assumed transferred authorities from other federal agencies on July 21, 2011. The CFPB is an independent agency, and is funded by a quarterly transfer of funds from the combined earnings of the Federal Reserve System. The Director of the CFPB serves on the FDIC Board of Directors and the Financial Stability Oversight Council.

The CFPB seeks to foster a consumer financial marketplace where customers can clearly see prices and risks up front and can easily make product comparisons; in which no one can build a business model around unfair, deceptive, or abusive practices; and that works for American consumers, responsible providers, and the economy as a whole. To accomplish this, the CFPB works to help consumer financial markets operate by making rules more effective, by consistently and fairly enforcing those rules, and by empowering consumers to take more control over their economic lives.

The Dodd-Frank Act sets forth the following functions for the CFPB:

- conducting financial education programs;
- collecting, investigating, and responding to consumer complaints;
- collecting, researching, monitoring, and publishing information relevant to the identification of risks to consumers and the proper functioning of financial markets;
- issuing rules, orders, and guidance implementing federal consumer financial laws;
- taking appropriate enforcement action to address violations of federal consumer financial laws; and
- supervising covered entities to assess compliance with federal consumer financial laws and detect financial risks to consumers.

The CFPB has statutory authority to conduct examinations to ensure that consumer financial products and services conform to federal consumer financial laws, and for related purposes. The CFPB's supervision program oversees:

- Insured depository entities with total assets over $10 billion and their affiliates. These institutions collectively hold more than 80 percent of the banking industry's assets.

- Certain nondepository entities regardless of size—mortgage companies (originators, brokers, and servicers, as well as related loan modification or foreclosure relief services firms), payday lenders, and private education lenders. CFPB can also supervise through rulemaking the larger players, or "larger participants," in consumer financial markets, and any nondepository entity nonbank that it determines is posing a risk to consumers in connection with the offering or provision of consumer financial products or services.

The CFPB's supervisory activities are conducted by the Division of Supervision, Enforcement, Fair Lending and Equal Opportunity. The division is headquartered in Washington, D.C., with regional offices in San Francisco (West), Chicago (Midwest), New York (Northeast), and Washington, D.C. (Southeast). Examination staff is assigned to one of the four regions.

Federal Deposit Insurance Corporation

Congress created the Federal Deposit Insurance Corporation (FDIC or Corporation) in 1933 to promote stability and public confidence in our nation's banking system. The FDIC accomplishes its mission by insuring deposits, examining and supervising financial institutions for safety and soundness and consumer protection, and managing receiverships. In its unique role as deposit insurer, the FDIC works in cooperation with other federal and state regulatory agencies to identify, monitor, and address risks to the Deposit Insurance Fund (DIF) posed by insured depository institutions.

Management of the FDIC is vested in a five-member Board of Directors. No more than three board members may be of the same political party. Three of the directors are directly appointed by the President, with the advice and consent of the Senate, for six-year terms. One of the three appointed directors is designated by the President as Chairman for a term of five years, and another is designated as Vice Chairman. The other two board members are the Comptroller of the Currency and the Director of the CFPB.

The FDIC's operations are organized into three major program areas: insurance, supervision, and receivership management. A description of each of these areas follows:

Insurance: The FDIC maintains stability and public confidence in the U.S. financial system by providing deposit insurance. As insurer, the Corporation must continually evaluate and effectively manage how changes in the economy, the financial markets, and the banking system affect the adequacy and the viability of the DIF. When an insured depository institution fails, the FDIC ensures that the financial institution's customers have timely access to their insured deposits and other services.

The FDIC provides the public with a sound deposit insurance system by supplying comprehensive statistical information on banking; identifying and analyzing emerging risks; conducting research that supports deposit insurance, banking policy, and risk assessment; and assessing the adequacy of the DIF and maintaining an effective and fair risk-based premium system.

The Dodd-Frank Act revised the statutory authorities governing the FDIC's management of the DIF. As a result of these changes, the FDIC developed a comprehensive, long-range management plan for the DIF that sets an appropriate target fund size and a strategy for assessment rates and dividends. In October 2010, pursuant to the comprehensive plan, the FDIC adopted a new Restoration Plan to ensure that the reserve ratio reaches the statutory mandates required by the Dodd-Frank Act in a timely manner. The Dodd-Frank Act also required the FDIC to amend its regulations to define the assessment base as average consolidated total assets minus average tangible equity, rather than domestic deposits (which, with minor adjustments, it has been since 1935).

The FDIC continued its efforts to improve risk differentiation and reduce the pro-cyclicality of the deposit insurance assessment system by issuing a rule that revised the assessment system applicable to large insured depository institutions to better reflect risk in a timely manner, to better differentiate large institutions during periods of good economic conditions,

27

and to better take into account the losses that the FDIC may incur if such an institution fails. The rule became effective in April 2011.

Supervision: The FDIC has primary federal regulatory and supervisory authority over insured state-chartered banks that are not members of the Federal Reserve System and for state-chartered savings associations. In July 2011, pursuant to the Dodd-Frank Act, supervisory responsibilities for state-charted savings associations were transferred to the FDIC from the OTS, shortly before the latter agency was abolished. The FDIC also has backup examination and enforcement authority over all insured institutions. Accordingly, the FDIC can examine for insurance purposes any insured financial institution, either directly or in cooperation with state or other federal supervisory authorities. The FDIC can also recommend that the appropriate federal banking agency take action against an insured institution and may do so itself if it deems necessary. In addition, the Dodd-Frank Act expanded the FDIC's authority to manage the failure of systemically-significant firms.

The FDIC's supervisory activities for risk management and consumer protection are organized into six regional offices and two area offices. The regional offices are located in Atlanta, Chicago, Dallas, Kansas City, New York, and San Francisco. The two area offices are located in Boston (reports to New York) and Memphis (reports to Dallas). In addition to the regional and area offices, the FDIC maintains 86 field territory offices for risk-management and 76 field territory offices for compliance, with dedicated examiners assigned to many of the largest financial institutions.

Receivership Management: Bank resolutions are handled by the Division of Resolutions and Receiverships. In protecting insured deposits, the FDIC is charged with resolving failed depository institutions at the least possible cost to the DIF. In carrying out this responsibility, the FDIC engages in several activities, including paying off deposits, arranging the purchase of assets and assumption of liabilities of failed institutions, effecting insured deposit transfers between institutions, creating and operating temporary bridge banks until a resolution can be accomplished, and using its conservatorship powers.

Similarly, Title II of the Dodd-Frank Act vests the FDIC with authority to resolve a failing systemically-important financial company, including a bank holding company, if use of that authority would avoid or mitigate potential adverse consequences for the financial system, and complies with other statutory standards. Consistent with these responsibilities, as well as its role on the FSOC helping to promote financial stability, the Dodd-Frank Act also expanded the FDIC's backup examination authority to include certain bank holding companies and systemically-important financial companies designated by the FSOC for supervision by the FRB.

Recent Structural Changes

In 2011, the FDIC completed various structural changes to more effectively allocate its resources to address industry risks and to implement the Dodd-Frank Act. Structural changes included the following:

The Office of Complex Financial Institutions was created to oversee the condition and orderly liquidation of bank holding companies with more than $100 billion in assets, as well as systemically-important nonbank financial companies, designated by the FSOC.

The former Division of Supervision and Consumer Protection was separated into two divisions to more effectively focus on safety and soundness and consumer protection issues. The new Division of Risk Management Supervision oversees the safety and soundness of insured state non-member banks and savings associations with less than $100 billion in total assets. The Division of Depositor and Consumer Protection was established to centralize all of the FDIC's consumer protection functions, including the examination and enforcement programs, into one division. Under Dodd-Frank, the FDIC retained examination and enforcement authority for several laws and regulations including the Community Reinvestment Act without regard to the size of an institution. Examination and enforcement responsibilities were transferred to the CFPB for certain statutes enumerated in Dodd-Frank for institutions with assets of $10 billion or more and their banking affiliates.

The Office of Corporate Risk Management was established to assess external and internal risks faced by the FDIC, enhancing the Agency's existing risk management practices. When fully staffed, the Office of Corporate Risk Management will have a small core staff and will work with internal committees, risk-specific working groups, and front-line offices and divisions which will continue to be responsible for risk management. The new Office will play an advisory and supporting role and will identify risks that require consideration by senior management and the Board.

The Office of Minority and Women Inclusion was established

with responsibility for all matters
of the agency relating to diversity
in management, employment, and
business activities.

National Credit Union Administration

The National Credit Union Administration (NCUA), established by Congress in 1934 through section 1752a of the Federal Credit Union Act, is the independent federal agency that supervises the nation's federal credit union system. A three-member bipartisan board, appointed by the President for six-year terms, manages the NCUA. The President also selects one board member to serve as the Chairman.

The NCUA's main responsibilities are as follows:

- charter, regulate, and supervise more than 4,400 federal credit unions in the United States and its territories;

- administer the National Credit Union Share Insurance Fund (NCUSIF), which insures member share accounts in just under 7,100 federal and state-chartered credit unions;

- administer the Temporary Corporate Credit Union Stabilization Fund, which has borrowing authority from the U.S. Treasury and assessment authority to resolve corporate credit union issues; and

- manage the Central Liquidity Facility, created to improve the financial stability of credit unions by providing liquidity to the credit union system.

The NCUA also has statutory authority to examine and supervise NCUSIF-insured, state-chartered credit unions in coordination with state regulators.

The NCUA is headquartered in Alexandria, Virginia and has five regional offices across the United States to administer its responsibilities for chartering and supervising credit unions. Additionally, the Asset Management and Assistance Center located in Austin, Texas manages the recovery of assets for liquidated credit unions. NCUA examiners conduct on-site examinations and supervision of each federal credit union and selected state-chartered credit unions. The NCUA is funded by the credit unions it regulates and insures.

Office of the Comptroller of the Currency

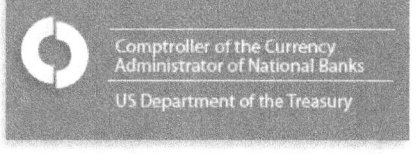

The Office of the Comptroller of the Currency (OCC) is the oldest federal bank regulatory agency, established as a bureau of the Treasury Department by the National Currency Act of 1863. It is headed by the Comptroller of the Currency, who is appointed to a five-year term by the President with the advice and consent of the Senate. The Comptroller is also a Director of the FDIC.

The OCC was created by Congress to charter, regulate, and supervise national banks. On July 21, 2011, pursuant to the Dodd-Frank Act, the OCC assumed supervisory responsibility for federal savings associations, as well as rulemaking authority relating to all savings associations.

The OCC regulates and supervises 1,400 national banks and trust companies, 637 federal savings associations, and 47 federal branches of foreign banks accounting for approximately 76 percent of the total assets of all U.S. commercial banks, federal savings associations, and branches of foreign banks. The OCC seeks to ensure that national banks and federal savings associations (collectively "banks") safely and soundly manage their risks, comply with applicable laws, compete effectively with other providers of financial services, offer products and services that meet the needs of customers, and provide fair access to financial services and fair treatment of their customers. The OCC's mission-critical programs include:

- chartering banks and issuing interpretations related to permissible banking activities;

- establishing and communicating regulations, policies, and operating guidance applicable to banks; and

- supervising the national system of banks and savings associations through on-site examinations, off-site monitoring, systemic risk analyses, and appropriate enforcement activities.

To meet its objectives, the OCC maintains a nationwide staff of bank examiners and other professional and support personnel. Headquartered in Washington, DC, the OCC has four district offices which are located in Chicago, Dallas, Denver, and New York. In addition, the OCC maintains a network of 73 field offices and 18 satellite locations in cities throughout the United States, as well as resident examiner teams in 24 of the largest national banking companies and an examining office in London, England.

The Comptroller receives advice on policy and operational issues from an Executive Committee, comprised of senior agency officials who lead major business units.

The OCC is funded primarily by semiannual assessments on banks, interest revenue from its investment in U.S. Treasury securities, and other fees. The OCC does not receive congressional appropriations for any of its operations.

ASSETS, LIABILITIES, AND NET WORTH of U.S. Commercial Banks, Thrift Institutions, and Credit Unions as of December 31, 2011[1]

Billions of dollars

Item	Total	U.S. Commercial Banks[2]			U.S. Branches and Agencies of Foreign Banks[5]	Thrift Institutions[4]		Credit Unions[3]	
		National	State Member	State Non-Member		OCC Regulated Federal Charter	FDIC Regulated State Charter[6]	Federal Charter	State Charter
Total assets	*16,955*	*8,732*	*1,886*	*2,016*	*2,117*	*917*	*325*	*526*	*436*
Total loans and receivables (net)	8,371	4,384	852	1,292	524	550	202	307	260
Loans secured by real estate[7]	4,476	2,228	497	812	33	412	181	165	149
Consumer loans[8]	1,566	916	68	228	0	93	5	145	111
Commercial and industrial loans	1,609	873	194	208	258	54	17	2	3
All other loans and lease receivables[9]	918	499	110	71	234	1	2	0	1
LESS: Allowance for possible loan and lease losses	201	133	19	27	0	10	3	5	4
Federal funds sold and securities purchased under agreements to resell	586	424	18	15	120	4	4	0	1
Cash and due from depository institutions[10]	2,122	699	342	155	744	13	24	77	69
Securities and other obligations[11]	3,200	1,702	436	401	147	240	70	119	86
U.S. government obligations[12]	821	202	71	84	47	181	55	106	75
Obligations of state and local governments[13]	217	103	34	69	0	6	6	0	0
Other securities	2,163	1,397	332	248	100	53	9	13	11
Other assets[14]	2,675	1,522	237	153	583	111	26	23	20
Total liabilities	*15,287*	*7,762*	*1,675*	*1,775*	*2,177*	*808*	*286*	*472*	*392*
Total deposits and shares[15]	11,947	6,231	1,460	1,559	942	683	245	449	378
Federal funds purchased and securities sold under agreements to repurchase	776	342	61	35	303	25	10	0	0
Other borrowings[16]	1,256	656	72	151	240	84	27	17	9
Other liabilities[17]	1,309	533	83	29	632	17	4	6	5
Net worth[18]	*1,669*	*970*	*211*	*241*	*1*	*109*	*39*	*54*	*44*
Memorandum: Number of institutions reporting	14,664	1,310	811	4,149	233	619	448	4,447	2,647

Footnotes to Tables

1. The table covers institutions, including those in Puerto Rico and U.S. territories and possessions, insured by the Federal Deposit Insurance Corporation or National Credit Union Savings Insurance Fund. All branches and agencies of foreign banks in the United States, but excluding any in Puerto Rico and U.S. territories and possessions, are covered whether or not insured. Excludes Edge Act and agreement corporations that are not subsidiaries of U.S. commercial banks.

2. Reflects fully consolidated statements of FDIC-insured U.S. banks—including their foreign branches, foreign subsidiaries, branches in Puerto Rico and U.S. territories and possessions, and FDIC insured banks in Puerto Rico and U.S. territories and possessions. Excludes bank holding companies.

3. Data are for federally insured natural person credit unions only.

4. Data for Thrift Institutions includes Stock Savings Banks, Mutual Savings Banks, Stock Savings & Loan Associations and Mutual Savings & Loan Associations that are Federally Chartered or State Chartered. Data for thrift institutions regulated by the OCC and FDIC are unconsolidated except for operating and finance subsidiaries.

5. These institutions are not required to file reports of income.

6. Includes State Chartered Thrift Institutions formerly regulated by the Office of Thrift Supervision.

7. Includes loans secured by residential property, commercial property, farmland (including improvements) and unimproved land; and construction loans secured by real estate.

8. Includes loans, except those secured by real estate, to individuals for household, family, and other personal expenditures including both installment and single payment loans. Net of unearned income on installment loans.

9. Includes loans to financial institutions, for purchasing or carrying securities, to finance agricultural production and other loans to farmers (except those secured by real estate), to states and political subdivisions and public authorities, and miscellaneous types of loans.

10. Includes vault cash, cash items in process of collection, and balances with U.S. and foreign banks and other depository institutions (including demand and time deposits and certifi-

Notes continue on the next page

INCOME AND EXPENSES of U.S. Commercial Banks, Thrift Institutions, and Credit Unions for the Twelve Months Ending December 31, 2011[1]

Billions of dollars

Item	Total	U.S. Commercial Banks[2]			Thrift Institutions[4]		Credit Unions[3]	
		National	State Member	State Non-Member	OCC Regulated Federal Charter	FDIC Regulated State Charter[6]	Federal Charter	State Charter
Operating income:	764	465	89	114	53	15	28	22
Interest and fees on loans	415	235	39	80	32	11	18	15
Other interest and dividend income	113	75	14	12	6	2	3	2
All other operating income	236	155	35	23	14	2	7	5
Operating expenses:	597	355	72	89	45	12	24	19
Salaries and benefits	184	114	25	25	8	4	8	7
Interest on deposits and shares	57	26	6	13	6	2	4	3
Interest on other borrowed money	32	19	3	4	4	1	1	0
Provision for loan and lease losses	78	48	8	13	6	1	2	2
All other operating expenses	243	147	31	33	20	4	9	7
Net operating income	*166*	*110*	*16*	*25*	*8*	*3*	*4*	*3*
Securities gains and losses	7	3	0	1	2	0	0	0
Extraordinary items	1	1	0	0	0	(0)	0	0
Income taxes	50	33	5	8	4	1	0	0
Net income	*124*	*81*	*11*	*19*	*7*	*2*	*4*	*3*
Memorandum: Number of institutions reporting	14,431	1,310	811	4,149	619	448	4,447	2,647

cates of deposit for all categories of institutions).

11. Includes government and corporate securities, including mortgage-backed securities and obligations of states and political subdivisions and of U.S. government agencies and corporations.

12. U.S. Treasury securities and securities of, and loans to, U.S. government agencies and corporations.

13. Securities issued by states and political subdivisions and public authorities, except for savings and loan associations and U.S. branches and agencies of foreign banks that do not report these securities separately. Loans to states and political subdivisions and public authorities are included in "All other loans and lease receivables."

14. Customers liabilities on acceptances, real property owned, various accrual accounts, and miscellaneous assets. For U.S. branches and agencies of foreign banks, also includes net due from head office and other related institutions.

15. Includes demand, savings, and time deposits, (including certificates of deposit at commercial banks, U.S. branches and agencies of foreign banks, and savings banks), credit balances at U.S. agencies of foreign banks and share balances at savings and loan associations and credit unions (including certificates of deposit, NOW accounts, and share draft accounts). For U.S. commercial banks, includes deposits in foreign offices, branches in U.S. territories and possessions, and Edge Act and Agreement corporation subsidiaries.

16. Includes interest-bearing demand notes issued to the U.S. Treasury, borrowing from Federal Reserve Banks and Federal Home Loan Banks, subordinated debt, limited life preferred stock, and other nondeposit borrowing.

17. Includes depository institutions own mortgage borrowing, liability for capitalized leases, liability on acceptances executed, various accrual accounts, and miscellaneous liabilities. For U.S. branches and agencies of foreign banks, also includes net owed to head office and other related institutions.

18. Includes capital stock, surplus, capital reserves, and undivided profits.

NOTE: Data are rounded to nearest billion. Consequently, some information may not reconcile precisely. Additionally, balances less than $500 million will show as zero.

APPENDIX A: RELEVANT STATUTES

Federal Financial Institutions Examination Council Act

12 U.S.C. § 3301. Declaration of purpose

It is the purpose of this chapter to establish a Financial Institutions Examination Council which shall prescribe uniform principles and standards for the Federal examination of financial institutions by the Office of the Comptroller of the Currency, the Federal Deposit Insurance Corporation, the Board of Governors of the Federal Reserve System, the Federal Home Loan Bank Board, and the National Credit Union Administration and make recommendations to promote uniformity in the supervision of these financial institutions. The Council's actions shall be designed to promote consistency in such examination and to insure progressive and vigilant supervision.

12 U.S.C. § 3302. Definitions

As used in this chapter—

(1) the term "Federal financial institutions regulatory agencies" means the Office of the Comptroller of the Currency, the Board of Governors of the Federal Reserve System, the Federal Deposit Insurance Corporation, the Office of Thrift Supervision, and the National Credit Union Administration;

(2) the term "Council" means the Financial Institutions Examination Council; and

(3) the term "financial institution" means a commercial bank, a savings bank, a trust company, a savings association, a building and loan association, a homestead association, a cooperative bank, or a credit union.

12 U.S.C. § 3303. Financial Institutions Examination Council

(a) Establishment; composition

There is established the Financial Institutions Examination Council which shall consist of—

(1) the Comptroller of the Currency,

(2) the Chairman of the Board of Directors of the Federal Deposit Insurance Corporation,

(3) a Governor of the Board of Governors of the Federal Reserve System designated by the Chairman of the Board,

(4) the **Director of the Consumer Financial Protection Bureau,**[1]

(5) the Chairman of the National Credit Union Administration Board; and

(6) the Chairman of the State Liaison Committee

(b) Chairmanship

The members of the Council shall select the first chairman of the Council. Thereafter the chairmanship shall rotate among the members of the Council.

(c) Term of office

---

1. The Dodd Frank Wall Street Reform and Consumer Protection Act of 2010 amended several provisions in the relevant statutes, including excerpts contained in this appendix. Changes are shown as bolded and italicized. The amendments relating to the Consumer Financial Protection Bureau became effective on July 21, 2011.

The term of the Chairman of the Council shall be two years.

(d) Designation of officers and employees

The members of the Council may, from time to time, designate other officers or employees of their respective agencies to carry out their duties on the Council.

(e) Compensation and expenses

Each member of the Council shall serve without additional compensation but shall be entitled to reasonable expenses incurred while carrying out his official duties as such a member.

12 U.S.C. § 3304. Costs and expenses of Council

One-fifth of the costs and expenses of the Council, including the salaries of its employees, shall be paid by each of the Federal financial institutions regulatory agencies. Annual assessments for such share shall be levied by the Council based upon its projected budget for the year, and additional assessments may be made during the year, if necessary.

12 U.S.C. § 3305. Functions of Council

(a) Establishment of principles and standards

The Council shall establish uniform principles and standards and report forms for the examination of financial institutions which shall be applied by the Federal financial institutions regulatory agencies.

(b) Making recommendations

regarding supervisory matters and adequacy of supervisory tools

(1) The Council shall make recommendations for uniformity in other supervisory matters, such as, but not limited to, classifying loans subject to country risk, identifying financial institutions in need of special supervisory attention, and evaluating the soundness of large loans that are shared by two or more financial institutions. In addition, the Council shall make recommendations regarding the adequacy of supervisory tools for determining the impact of holding company operations on the financial institutions within the holding company and shall consider the ability of supervisory agencies to discover possible fraud or questionable and illegal payments and practices which might occur in the operation of financial institutions or their holding companies.

(2) When a recommendation of the Council is found unacceptable by one or more of the applicable Federal financial institutions regulatory agencies, the agency or agencies shall submit to the Council, within a time period specified by the Council, a written statement of the reasons the recommendation is unacceptable.

(c) Development of uniform reporting system

The Council shall develop uniform reporting systems for federally supervised financial institutions, their holding companies, and non-financial institution subsidiaries of such institutions or holding companies. The authority to develop uniform reporting systems shall not restrict or amend the requirements of section 78l(i) of Title 15.

(d) Conducting schools for examiners and assistant examiners

The Council shall conduct schools for examiners and assistant examiners employed by the Federal financial institutions regulatory agencies. Such schools shall be open to enrollment by employees of State financial institutions supervisory agencies and employees of the Federal Housing Finance Board under conditions specified by the Council.

(e) Affect on Federal regulatory agency research and development of new financial institutions supervisory agencies

Nothing in this chapter shall be construed to limit or discourage Federal regulatory agency research and development of new financial institutions supervisory methods and tools, nor to preclude the field testing of any innovation devised by any Federal regulatory agency.

(f) Annual report

Not later than April 1 of each year, the Council shall prepare an annual report covering its activities during the preceding year.

(g) Flood insurance

The Council shall consult with and assist the Federal entities for lending regulation, as such term is defined in section 4121(a) of Title 42, in developing and coordinating uniform standards and requirements for use by regulated lending institutions under the national flood insurance program.

12 U.S.C. § 3306. State liaison

To encourage the application of uniform examination principles and standards by State and Federal supervisory agencies, the Council shall establish a liaison committee composed of five representatives of State agencies which supervise financial institutions which shall meet at least

twice a year with the Council. Members of the liaison committee shall receive a reasonable allowance for necessary expenses incurred in attending meetings.

Members of the Liaison Committee shall elect a chairperson from among the members serving on the committee.

12 U.S.C. § 3307. Administration

(a) Authority of Chairman of Council

The Chairman of the Council is authorized to carry out and to delegate the authority to carry out the internal administration of the Council, including the appointment and supervision of employees and the distribution of business among members, employees, and administrative units.

(b) Use of personnel, services, and facilities of Federal financial institutions regulatory agencies, Federal Reserve banks, and Federal Home Loan Banks.

In addition to any other authority conferred upon it by this chapter, in carrying out its functions under this chapter, the Council may utilize, with their consent and to the extent practical, the personnel, services, and facilities of the Federal financial institutions regulatory agencies, Federal Reserve banks, and Federal Home Loan Banks, with or without reimbursement therefore.

(c) Compensation, authority, and duties of officers and employees; experts and consultants

In addition, the Council may—

(1) subject to the provisions of Title 5 relating to the competitive service, classification, and General Schedule pay rates, appoint and fix the compensation of such officers and employees as are necessary to

carry out the provisions of this chapter, and to prescribe the authority and duties of such officers and employees; and (2) obtain the services of such experts and consultants as are necessary to carry out the provisions of this chapter.

12 U.S.C. § 3308. Access to books, accounts, records, etc., by Council

For the purpose of carrying out this chapter, the Council shall have access to all books, accounts, records, reports, files, memorandums, papers, things, and property belonging to or in use by Federal financial institutions regulatory agencies, including reports of examination of financial institutions or their holding companies from whatever source, together with workpapers and correspondence files related to such reports, whether or not a part of the report, and all without any deletions.

12 U.S.C. § 3309. Risk management training

(a) Seminars

The Council shall develop and administer training seminars in risk management for its employees and the employees of insured financial institutions.

(b) Study of risk management training program

Not later than end of the 1-year period beginning on August 9, 1989, the Council shall—

(1) conduct a study on the feasibility and appropriateness of establishing a formalized risk management training program designed to lead to the certification of Risk Management Analysts; and

(2) report to the Congress the results of such study.

12 U.S.C. § 3310. Establishment of Appraisal Subcommittee

There shall be within the Council a subcommittee to be known as the "Appraisal Subcommittee," which shall consist of the designees of the heads of the Federal financial institutions regulatory agencies, the *Bureau of Consumer Financial Protection, and the Federal Housing Finance Agency*. Each such designee shall be a person who has demonstrated knowledge and competence concerning the appraisal profession. *At all times at least one member of the Appraisal Subcommittee shall have demonstrated knowledge and competence through licensure, certification, or professional designation within the appraisal profession.*

12 U.S.C. § 3311. Required review of regulations

(a) In general

Not less frequently than once every 10 years, the Council and each appropriate Federal banking agency represented on the Council shall conduct a review of all regulations prescribed by the Council or by any such appropriate Federal banking agency, respectively, in order to identify outdated or otherwise unnecessary regulatory requirements imposed on insured depository institutions.

(b) Process

In conducting the review under subsection (a) of this section, the Council or the appropriate Federal banking agency shall—

(1) categorize the regulations described in subsection (a) of this section by type (such as consumer regulations, safety and soundness regulations, or such other designations as determined by the Council, or the appropriate Federal banking agency); and

(2) at regular intervals, provide notice and solicit public comment on a particular category or categories of regulations, requesting commentators to identify areas of the regulations that are outdated, unnecessary, or unduly burdensome.

(c) Complete review

The Council or the appropriate Federal banking agency shall ensure that the notice and comment period described in subsection (b)(2) of this section is conducted with respect to all regulations described in subsection (a) of this section not less frequently than once every 10 years.

(d) Regulatory response

The Council or the appropriate Federal banking agency shall—

(1) publish in the Federal Register a summary of the comments received under this section, identifying significant issues raised and providing comment on such issues; and

(2) eliminate unnecessary regulations to the extent that such action is appropriate.

(e) Report to Congress

Not later than 30 days after carrying out subsection (d)(1) of this section, the Council shall submit to the Congress a report, which shall include—

(1) a summary of any significant issues raised by public comments received by the Council and the appropriate Federal banking agencies under this section and the relative merits of such issues; and

(2) an analysis of whether the appropriate Federal banking agency involved is able to address the regulatory burdens associated with such issues by regulation, or whether such bur-

dens must be addressed by legislative action.

Excerpts from Statute Governing Appraisal Subcommittee

12 U.S.C. § 3332. Functions of Appraisal Subcommittee

(a) In general

The Appraisal Subcommittee shall—

(1) monitor the requirements established by States—

(A) for the certification and licensing of individuals who are qualified to perform appraisals in connection with federally related transactions, including a code of professional responsibility; and

(B) for the registration and supervision of the operations and activities of an appraisal management company; and

(2) monitor the requirements established by the Federal financial institutions regulatory agencies with respect to—

(A) appraisal standards for federally related transactions under their jurisdiction, and

(B) determinations as to which federally related transactions under their jurisdiction require the services of a State certified appraiser and which require the services of a State licensed appraiser;

(3) maintain a national registry of State certified and licensed appraisers who are eligible to perform appraisals in federally related transactions; and

(4) Omitted.

(5) transmit an annual report to the Congress not later than June 15 of each year that describes the manner in which each function assigned to the Appraisal Subcommittee has been carried out during the preceding year. The report shall also detail the activities of the Appraisal Subcommittee, including the results of all audits of State appraiser regulatory agencies, and provide an accounting of disapproved actions and warnings taken in the previous year, including a description of the conditions causing the disapproval and actions taken to achieve compliance.

(6) maintain a national registry of appraisal management companies that either are registered with and subject to supervision of a State appraiser certifying and licensing agency or are operating subsidiaries of a Federally regulated financial institution.

(b) Monitoring and reviewing Foundation

The Appraisal Subcommittee shall monitor and review the practices, procedures, activities, and organizational structure of the Appraisal Foundation.

12 U.S.C. § 3333. Chairperson of Appraisal Subcommittee; term of Chairperson; meetings

(a) Chairperson

The Council shall select the Chairperson of the subcommittee. The term of the Chairperson shall be two years.

(b) Meetings; quorum; voting

The Appraisal Subcommittee shall *meet in public session after notice in the* **Federal Register,** *but may close certain portions of these meetings related to personnel and review of preliminary State audit reports,* at the call of the Chairperson or a majority of its members when there is business to be conducted. A majority of members of the Appraisal Subcommittee shall constitute a quorum but 2 or more members may hold hearings. Decisions of the Appraisal Subcommittee shall be made by the vote of a majority of its members. *The subject matter discussed in any closed or executive session shall be described in the* **Federal Register** *notice of the meeting.*

Excerpts from Home Mortgage Disclosure Act

12 U.S.C. § 2801. Congressional findings and declaration of purpose

(a) Findings of Congress

The Congress finds that some depository institutions have sometimes contributed to the decline of certain geographic areas by their failure pursuant to their chartering responsibilities to provide adequate home financing to qualified applicants on reasonable terms and conditions.

(b) Purpose of chapter

The purpose of this chapter is to provide the citizens and public officials of the United States with sufficient information to enable them to determine whether depository institutions are filling their obligations to serve the housing needs of the communities and neighborhoods in which they are located and to assist public officials in their determination of the distribution of public sector investments in a manner designed to improve the private investment environment.

(c) Construction of chapter

Nothing in this chapter is intended to, nor shall it be construed to, encourage unsound lending practices or the allocation of credit.

* * * * *

12 U.S.C. § 2803. Maintenance of records and public disclosure

* * *

(f) Data disclosure system; operation, etc.

The Federal Financial Institutions Examination Council, in consultation with the Secretary, shall implement a system to facilitate access to data required to be disclosed under this section. Such system shall include arrangements for a central depository of data in each primary metropolitan statistical area, metropolitan statistical area, or consolidated metropolitan statistical area that is not comprised of designated primary metropolitan statistical areas. Disclosure statements shall be made available to the public for inspection and copying at such central depository of data for all depository institutions which are required to disclose information under this section (or which are exempted pursuant to section

2805(b) of this title) and which have a home office or branch office within such primary metropolitan statistical area, metropolitan statistical area, or consolidated metropolitan statistical area that is not comprised of designated primary metropolitan statistical areas.

* * * * *

12 U.S.C. § 2809. Compilation of aggregate data

(a) Commencement; scope of data and tables

Beginning with data for calendar year 1980, the Federal Financial Institutions Examination Council shall compile each year, for each primary metropolitan statistical area, metropolitan statistical area, or consolidated metropolitan statistical area that is not comprised of designated primary metropolitan statistical areas, aggregate data by census tract for all depository institutions which are required to disclose data under section 2803 of this title or which are exempt pursuant to section 2805(b) of this

title. The Council shall also produce tables indicating, for each primary metropolitan statistical area, metropolitan statistical area, or consolidated metropolitan statistical area that is not comprised of designated primary metropolitan statistical areas, aggregate lending patterns for various categories of census tracts grouped according to location, age of housing stock, income level, and racial characteristics.

(b) Staff and data processing resources

The Board shall provide staff and data processing resources to the Council to enable it to carry out the provisions of subsection (a) of this section.

(c) Availability to public

The data and tables required pursuant to subsection (a) of this section shall be made available to the public no later than December 31 of the year following the calendar year on which the data is based.

Deloitte.

Deloitte & Touche LLP
Suite 800
1750 Tysons Boulevard
McLean, VA 22102-4219
USA

Tel: +1 703 251 1000
Fax: +1 703 251 3400
www.deloitte.com

INDEPENDENT AUDITORS' REPORT

To the Federal Financial Institutions Examination Council:
Washington, D C

We have audited the accompanying balance sheets of the Federal Financial Institutions
Examination Council (the "Council") as of December 31, 2011 and 2010, and the related
statements of revenues and expenses and changes in cumulative results of operations, and cash
flows for the years then ended   These financial statements are the responsibility of the Council's
management   Our responsibility is to express an opinion on these financial statements based on
our audits

We conducted our audits in accordance with auditing standards generally accepted in the United
States of America and the standards applicable to financial audits contained in *Government
Auditing Standards* issued by the Comptroller General of the United States   Those standards
require that we plan and perform the audit to obtain reasonable assurance about whether the
financial statements are free of material misstatement   An audit includes consideration of
internal control over financial reporting as a basis for designing audit procedures that are
appropriate in the circumstances, but not for the purpose of expressing an opinion on the
effectiveness of the Council's internal control over financial reporting   Accordingly, we express
no such opinion   An audit also includes examining, on a test basis, evidence supporting the
amounts and disclosures in the financial statements, assessing the accounting principles used and
significant estimates made by management, as well as evaluating the overall financial statement
presentation   We believe that our audits provide a reasonable basis for our opinion

In our opinion, such financial statements present fairly, in all material respects, the financial
position of the Federal Financial Institutions Examination Council as of December 31, 2011 and
2010, and the results of its operations and its cash flows for the years then ended in conformity
with accounting principles generally accepted in the United States of America

In accordance with *Government Auditing Standards*, we have also issued our report dated March
5, 2012, on our consideration of the Council's internal control over financial reporting and our
tests of its compliance with certain provisions of laws, regulations, contracts, and grant
agreements and other matters   The purpose of that report is to describe the scope of our testing
of internal control over financial reporting and compliance and the results of that testing, and not
to provide an opinion on the internal control over financial reporting or on compliance   That
report is an integral part of an audit performed in accordance with *Government Auditing
Standards* and should be considered in assessing the results of our audit

Deloitte + Touche LLP

March 5, 2012

Member of
Deloitte Touche Tohmatsu

FEDERAL FINANCIAL INSTITUTIONS EXAMINATION COUNCIL
Balance Sheets

	As of December 31,	
	2011	2010

ASSETS
CURRENT ASSETS

Cash	$ 543,453	$ 746,815
Accounts receivable from member organizations	785,708	1,276,250
Other accounts receivable—net	91,520	104,441
Total current assets	1,420,681	2,127,506

NONCURRENT ASSETS

Furniture and equipment—at cost	20,999	20,999
Furniture and equipment leased—at cost	198,485	198,485
Central Data Repository software—at cost	20,120,566	19,371,661
Home Mortgage Disclosure Act software—at cost	2,783,868	2,783,868
Less accumulated depreciation	(15,574,489)	(12,704,895)
Net capital assets	7,549,429	9,670,118
TOTAL ASSETS	$ 8,970,110	$ 11,797,624

LIABILITIES AND CUMULATIVE RESULTS OF OPERATIONS

CURRENT LIABILITIES

Accounts payable and accrued liabilities payable to member organizations	$ 805,796	$ 839,152
Other accounts payable and accrued liabilities	285,947	988,059
Accrued annual leave	22,971	27,746
Capital lease payable	39,376	37,828
Deferred revenue	3,125,930	2,746,667
Total current liabilities	4,280,020	4,639,452

LONG-TERM LIABILITIES

Capital lease payable	102,825	142,202
Deferred revenue	4,285,874	6,746,128
Deferred rent	9,996	6,605
Total long-term liabilities	4,398,695	6,894,935
Total liabilities	8,678,715	11,534,387
CUMULATIVE RESULTS OF OPERATIONS	291,395	263,237
TOTAL LIABILITIES AND CUMULATIVE RESULTS OF OPERATIONS	$ 8,970,110	$ 11,797,624

See notes to financial statements.

FEDERAL FINANCIAL INSTITUTIONS EXAMINATION COUNCIL
Statements of Revenues and Expenses and Changes in Cumulative Results of Operations

	For the years ended December 31,	
	2011	2010
REVENUES		
Assessments on member organizations	$ 687,107	$ 632,344
Central Data Repository	4,936,912	4,452,286
Home Mortgage Disclosure Act	3,727,927	3,433,075
Tuition	3,246,549	2,662,193
Community Reinvestment Act	946,928	1,024,844
Uniform Bank Performance Report	351,646	464,633
Total revenues	13,897,069	12,669,375
EXPENSES		
Data processing	4,164,479	4,529,275
Professional fees	4,121,224	3,635,374
Salaries and related benefits	1,781,660	1,739,031
Depreciation	2,869,594	1,877,343
Rental of office space	264,989	264,989
Adminstration fees	281,000	245,000
Travel	242,659	170,404
Other seminar expenses	33,526	30,297
Rental and maintenance of office equipment	27,544	48,313
Office and other supplies	56,237	25,033
Printing	18,389	18,380
Postage	2,564	1,660
Miscellaneous	5,046	7,021
Total expenses	13,868,911	12,592,120
RESULTS OF OPERATIONS	28,158	77,255
CUMULATIVE RESULTS OF OPERATIONS—Beginning of year	263,237	185,982
CUMULATIVE RESULTS OF OPERATIONS—End of year	$ 291,395	$ 263,237

See notes to financial statements.

FEDERAL FINANCIAL INSTITUTIONS EXAMINATION COUNCIL
Statements of Cash Flows

	For the years ended December 31,	
	2011	2010
CASH FLOWS FROM OPERATING ACTIVITIES		
Results of operations	$ 28,158	$ 77,255
Adjustments to reconcile results of operations to net cash provided by operating activities:		
Depreciation	2,869,594	1,877,343
(Increase) decrease in assets:		
Accounts receivable from member organizations	490,542	(275,247)
Other accounts receivable	12,921	(13,812)
Increase (decrease) in liabilities:		
Accounts payable and accured liabilities payable to member organizations	(33,356)	(77,379)
Other accounts payable and accrued liabilities	(284,515)	(162,453)
Accrued annual leave	(4,775)	7,629
Deferred revenue (current and non-current)	(2,080,991)	(276,603)
Deferred rent	3,391	6,605
Net cash provided by operating activities	1,000,969	1,163,338
CASH FLOWS FROM INVESTING ACTIVITIES		
Capital expenditures	(1,169,016)	(1,427,853)
CASH FLOWS FROM FINANCING ACTIVITIES		
Capital lease payments	(35,315)	(11,370)
NET INCREASE (DECREASE) IN CASH	(203,362)	(275,885)
CASH BALANCE—Beginning of year	746,815	1,022,700
CASH BALANCE—End of year	$ 543,453	$ 746,815

See notes to financial statements.

Notes to Financial Statements as of and for the Years Ended December 31, 2011 and 2010

1. Organization and Purpose

The Federal Financial Institutions Examination Council (the Council) was established under Title X of the Financial Institutions Regulatory and Interest Rate Control Act of 1978. The purpose of the Council is to prescribe uniform principles and standards for the federal examination of financial institutions and to make recommendations to promote uniformity in the supervision of these financial institutions. The five agencies which were represented on the Council during 2011, referred to hereinafter as member organizations, are as follows:

> Board of Governors of the Federal Reserve System (FRB)
> Consumer Financial Protection Bureau (CFPB)
> Federal Deposit Insurance Corporation (FDIC)
> National Credit Union Administration (NCUA)
> Office of the Comptroller of the Currency (OCC)

In accordance with the Financial Services Regulatory Relief Act of 2006, a representative state regulator was added as a full voting member of the Council in October 2006.

The Council was given additional statutory responsibilities by section 340 of the Housing and Community Development Act of 1980, Public Law 96-399. Among these responsibilities are the implementation of a system to facilitate public access to data that depository institutions must disclose under the Home Mortgage Disclosure Act of 1975 (HMDA) and the aggregation of annual HMDA data, by census tract, for each metropolitan statistical area.

On July 21, 2010, the Dodd-Frank Wall Street Reform and Consumer Protection Act of 2010 (Dodd-Frank Act) was signed into law. This legislation substitutes the director of the Consumer Financial Protection Bureau for the director of the Office of Thrift Supervision (OTS) as a member of the Council effective July 21, 2011.

The Council's financial statements do not include financial data for the Council's Appraisal Subcommittee (the Subcommittee). The Subcommittee was created pursuant to Public Law 101–73, Title XI of the Financial Institutions Reform, Recovery, and Enforcement Act of 1989. Although it is a subcommittee of the Council, the Appraisal Subcommittee maintains separate financial records and administrative processes. The Council is not responsible for any debts incurred by the Subcommittee, nor are Subcommittee funds available for use by the Council.

2. Significant Accounting Policies

The Council prepares its financial statements in accordance with accounting principles generally accepted in the United States of America (GAAP).

Revenues—Assessments are made on member organizations to fund the Council s operations based on expected cash needs. Amounts over- or under- assessed due to differences between actual and expected cash needs are presented in the "Cumulative Results of Operations" line item during the year and then are used to offset or increase the next year's assessment. Deficits in "Cumulative Results of Operations" can be recouped in the following year's assessments.

The Council provides seminars in the Washington, D.C. area and at locations throughout the country for member organizations and other agencies. The Council also coordinates the production and distribution of the Uniform Bank Performance Reports (UBPR) through the FDIC. Tuition and UBPR revenue is adjusted at year-end to match expenses incurred as a result of providing education classes and UBPR services. For differences between revenues and expenses, member agencies are assessed an additional amount or credited a refund based on each member's proportional cost for the Examiner Education and UBPR budget. The Council also recognizes revenue from member agencies for expenses incurred related to the Community Reinvestment Act.

Capital Assets—Furniture and equipment is recorded at cost less accumulated depreciation. Depreciation is calculated on a straight-line basis over the estimated useful lives of the assets, which range from four to ten years. Upon the sale or other disposition of a depreciable asset, the cost and related accumulated depreciation are removed and any gain or loss is recognized. The Central Data Repository (CDR) and the HMDA rewrite, internally developed software projects, are recorded at cost as required by the Internal Use Software Topic of Financial Accounting Standards Board (FASB) Accounting Standards Codification.

Deferred Revenue—Deferred revenue includes cash collected and accounts receivable related to the CDR and HMDA.

Deferred Rent—The lease for office and classroom space contains scheduled rent increases over the term of the lease. As required by the Leases Topic of the FASB Accounting Standards Codification, rent abatements and scheduled rent increases must be considered in determining the annual rent expense to be recognized. The deferred rent represents the difference between the actual lease payments and the rent expense recognized.

Estimates—The preparation of financial statements in conformity with GAAP requires management to make estimates and assumptions that affect the reported amounts of assets and liabilities and the disclosure of contingent assets and liabilities at the date of the financial statements and the reported amounts of revenues and expenses during the reporting period. Actual results could differ from those estimates.

Allowance for Doubtful Accounts—Accounts receivable for non-members are shown net of the allowance for doubtful accounts. Accounts receivable considered uncollectible are charged against the allowance account in the year they are deemed uncollectible. The allowance for doubtful accounts is adjusted monthly, based upon a review of outstanding receivables.

3. Transactions with Member Organizations

	2011	2010
Accounts Receivable		
Board of Governors of the Federal Reserve System	$ 132,539	$ 290,047
Consumer Financial Protection Bureau	0	0
Federal Deposit Insurance Corporation	194,230	467,726
National Credit Union Administration	46,051	47,501
Office of the Comptroller of the Currency	412,888	416,572
	$ 785,708	$1,221,846
Accounts Payable and Accrued Liabilities		
Board of Governors of the Federal Reserve System	$ 494,234	$ 579,792
Consumer Financial Protection Bureau	0	0
Federal Deposit Insurance Corporation	175,940	126,265
National Credit Union Administration	27,080	7,624
Office of the Comptroller of the Currency	108,542	124,321
	$ 805,796	$ 838,002
Operations		
Council operating expenses reimbursed by members	$ 687,107	$ 632,344
FRB-provided administrative support	$ 281,000	$ 245,000
FRB-provided data processing	$ 4,164,479	$ 4,529,275

Notes continue on the following page.

The Council does not directly employ personnel, but rather member organizations detail personnel to support Council operations. These personnel are paid through the payroll systems of member organizations. Salaries and fringe benefits, including retirement benefit plan contributions, are reimbursed to these organizations. The Council does not have any post-retirement or post-employment benefit liabilities since Council personnel are included in the plans of the member organizations. Due to organizational changes resulting from the Dodd-Frank Act, the OCC absorbed all financial related activity of the OTS on July 21, 2011. As of December 31, 2010, the OTS had accounts receivable of $54,404 and accounts payable and accrued liabilities of $1,150 that are not reflected in the table above. These amounts were settled by and with the OTS during 2011 and thus were no longer outstanding as of December 31, 2011.

Member organizations are not reimbursed for the costs of personnel who serve as Council members and on the various task forces and committees of the Council. The value of these contributed services is not included in the accompanying financial statements.

4. Central Data Repository Software

In 2003, the Council entered into an agreement with UNISYS to enhance the methods and systems used to collect, validate, process, and distribute Call Report information, and to store this information in CDR. The CDR was placed into service in October 2005. At that time, the Council began depreciating the CDR project on the straight-line basis over its estimated useful life of 63 months. In 2009, the Council reevaluated the useful life of CDR and decided to extend the estimated useful life by an additional 36 months based on enhanced functionality of the software. The Council records depreciation expenses and recognizes the same amount of revenue. The value of the CDR asset as of December 31, 2011 and 2010, includes the fully accrued and paid cost.

Capital Asset CDR	2011	2010
Beginning balance	$19,371,661	$18,231,272
Software placed in use during the year	748,905	1,140,389
Total asset	$20,120,566	$19,371,661

Accounts Payable and Accrued Liabilities Related to CDR

	2011	2010
Payable to UNISYS for the CDR project	$ 216,012	$ 865,630

CDR *Revenues* — The Council is funding the project by billing the three participating Council member organizations (FRB, FDIC, and OCC). Funding for the years ended December 31, 2011 and 2010, is as follows:

Deferred Revenue	2011	2010
Beginning balance	$ 6,708,927	$ 7,424,718
Additions	748,906	1,140,389
Less revenue recognized	(2,319,521)	(1,856,180)
Ending balance	$ 5,138,312	$ 6,708,927
Current portion deferred revenue	$ 2,569,156	$ 2,236,309
Long-term deferred revenue	2,569,156	4,472,618
Total Deferred Revenue	$ 5,138,312	$ 6,708,927

Total CDR Revenue		
Deferred revenue recognized	$ 2,319,521	$ 1,856,180
Hosting and maintenance revenue	2,617,391	2,596,106
Total CDR Revenue	$ 4,936,912	$ 4,452,286

Depreciation		
Depreciation for the CDR project	$ 2,319,521	$ 1,856,180
Average monthly depreciation	$ 193,293	$ 154,682

5. Home Mortgage Disclosure Act Software

The Council entered into an agreement with FRB to maintain and support the HMDA processing system. In 2007, the Council began a rewrite of the entire HMDA processing system, which went into service in 2011. The Council began depreciating the HMDA project on the straight-line basis over its estimated useful life of 60 months. The financial activity associated with the processing system for the years ended December 31, 2011 and 2010, is as follows:

Deferred Revenue	2011	2010
Beginning balance	$ 2,783,868	$ 2,344,680
Additions	0	439,188
Less revenue recognized	(510,376)	0
Ending balance	$ 2,273,492	$ 2,783,868
Current portion deferred revenue	$ 556,774	$ 510,358
Long-term deferred revenue	1,716,718	2,273,510
Total Deferred Revenue	$ 2,273,492	$ 2,783,868

	2011	2010

Total HMDA Revenue

The Council recognized the following revenue from member organizations for the production and distribution of reports under the HMDA; includes the deferred revenue recognized in 2011: $ 2,857,085 $ 2,537,870

The Council recognized the following revenue from the Department of Housing and Urban Development s participation in the HMDA project: 556,207 588,421

The Council recognized the following revenue from the Mortgage Insurance Companies of America for performing HMDA-related work: 314,635 306,784

Total HMDA	$ 3,727,927	$ 3,433,075

Depreciation		
Depreciation for the HMDA Rewrite project	$ 510,376	$ 0
Average monthly depreciation	$ 46,398	$ 0

6. Operating Leases

The FRB, on behalf of the Council, entered into an operating lease at market value with the FDIC in January 2010 to secure office and classroom space.

Years ending December 31	Amount
2012	$ 264,900
2013	268,292
2014	271,772
Total minimum lease payments	$ 804,964

Rental expenses under this operating lease were $264,989 and $264,989 as of December 31, 2011 and 2010, respectively.

7. Capital Leases

In December 2009 and November 2010, the Council entered into capital leases for printing equipment. Furniture and equipment includes $198,485 for the capital leases. Accumulated depreciation is $60,860 and $21,163 for 2011 and 2010, respectively. Contingent rentals for excess usage of the printing equipment amounted to $13,531 and $11,049 in 2011 and 2010, respectively.

The future minimum lease payments required under the capital leases and the present value of the net minimum lease payments as of December 31, 2011, are as follows:

Years ending December 31	Amount
2012	$ 59,089
2013	59,089
2014	59,089
2015	31,736
Total minimum lease payments	209,003
Less amount representing maintenance	(57,761)
Net minimum lease payments	151,242
Less amount representing interest	(9,041)
Net minimum lease payments	142,201
Less current maturities of capital lease payments	(39,376)
Long-term capital lease obligations	$ 102,825

8. Subsequent Events

There were no subsequent events that require adjustments to or disclosures in the financial statements as of December 31, 2011. Subsequent events were evaluated through March 5, 2012, which is the date the financial statements were available to be issued.

Deloitte

Deloitte & Touche LLP
Suite 800
1750 Tysons Boulevard
McLean, VA 22102-4219
USA

Tel: +1 703 251 1000
Fax: +1 703 251 3400
www.deloitte.com

INDEPENDENT AUDITORS' REPORT ON INTERNAL CONTROL OVER FINANCIAL REPORTING AND ON COMPLIANCE AND OTHER MATTERS BASED ON AN AUDIT OF FINANCIAL STATEMENTS PERFORMED IN ACCORDANCE WITH GOVERNMENT AUDITING STANDARDS

To the Federal Financial Institutions Examination Council:
Washington, D C

We have audited the financial statements of the Federal Financial Institutions Examination Council (the "Council") as of and for the years ended December 31, 2011 and 2010, and have issued our report thereon dated March 5, 2012 We conducted our audit in accordance with auditing standards generally accepted in the United States of America and the standards applicable to financial audits contained in *Government Auditing Standards*, issued by the Comptroller General of the United States

Internal Control over Financial Reporting

Management of the Council is responsible for establishing and maintaining effective internal control over financial reporting In planning and performing our audit, we considered the Council's internal control over financial reporting as a basis for designing our auditing procedures for the purpose of expressing our opinion on the financial statements, but not for the purpose of expressing an opinion on the effectiveness of the Council's internal control over financial reporting Accordingly, we do not express an opinion on the effectiveness of the Council's internal control over financial reporting

A deficiency in internal control over financial reporting exists when the design or operation of a control does not allow management or employees, in the normal course of performing their assigned functions, to prevent or detect misstatements on a timely basis A significant deficiency is a deficiency, or combination of deficiencies, in internal control over financial reporting that is less severe than a material weakness, yet important enough to merit attention by those responsible for oversight of the Council's financial reporting A material weakness is a deficiency, or combination of deficiencies, in internal control over financial reporting, such that there is a reasonable possibility that a material misstatement of the Council's financial statements will not be prevented or detected on a timely basis

Our consideration of internal control over financial reporting was for the limited purpose described in the first paragraph of this section and was not designed to identify all deficiencies in internal control over financial reporting that might be deficiencies, significant deficiencies or material weaknesses We did not identify any deficiencies in internal control over financial reporting that we consider to be material weaknesses, as defined above

Member of
Deloitte Touche Tohmatsu

Compliance and Other Matters

As part of obtaining reasonable assurance about whether the Council's financial statements are free of material misstatement, we performed tests of its compliance with certain provisions of laws, regulations, contracts, and grant agreements, noncompliance with which could have a direct and material effect on the determination of financial statement amounts However, providing an opinion on compliance with those provisions was not an objective of our audit, and accordingly, we do not express such an opinion The results of our tests disclosed no instances of noncompliance or other matters that are required to be reported under *Government Auditing Standards.*

Distribution

This report is intended solely for the information and use of the Council, management, others within the organization, the Office of Inspector General, and the United States Congress, and is not intended to be and should not be used by anyone other than these specified parties

Deloitte + Touche LLP

March 5, 2012

APPENDIX C: MAPS OF AGENCY REGIONS AND DISTRICTS

THE FEDERAL RESERVE SYSTEM DISTRICTS

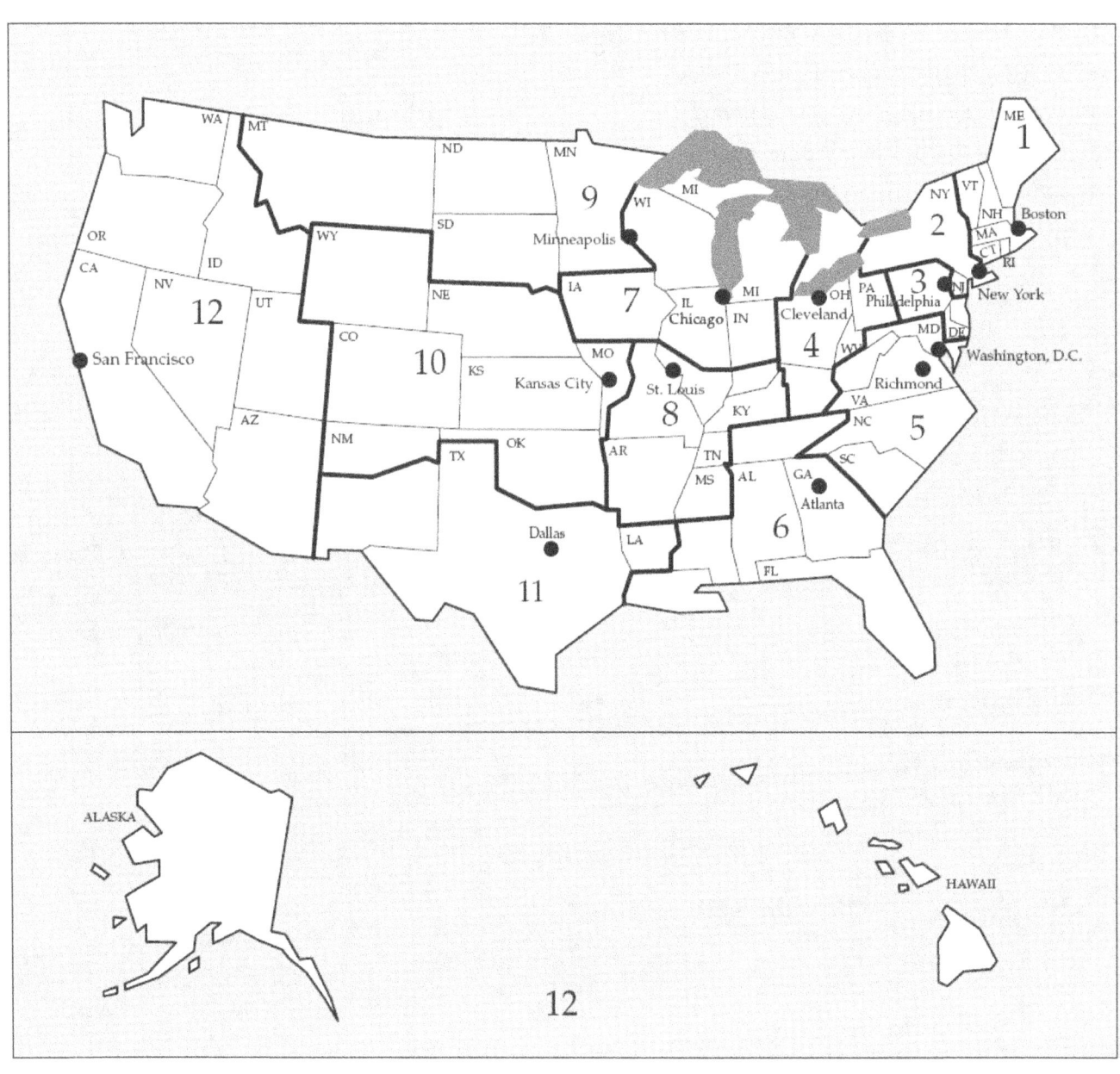

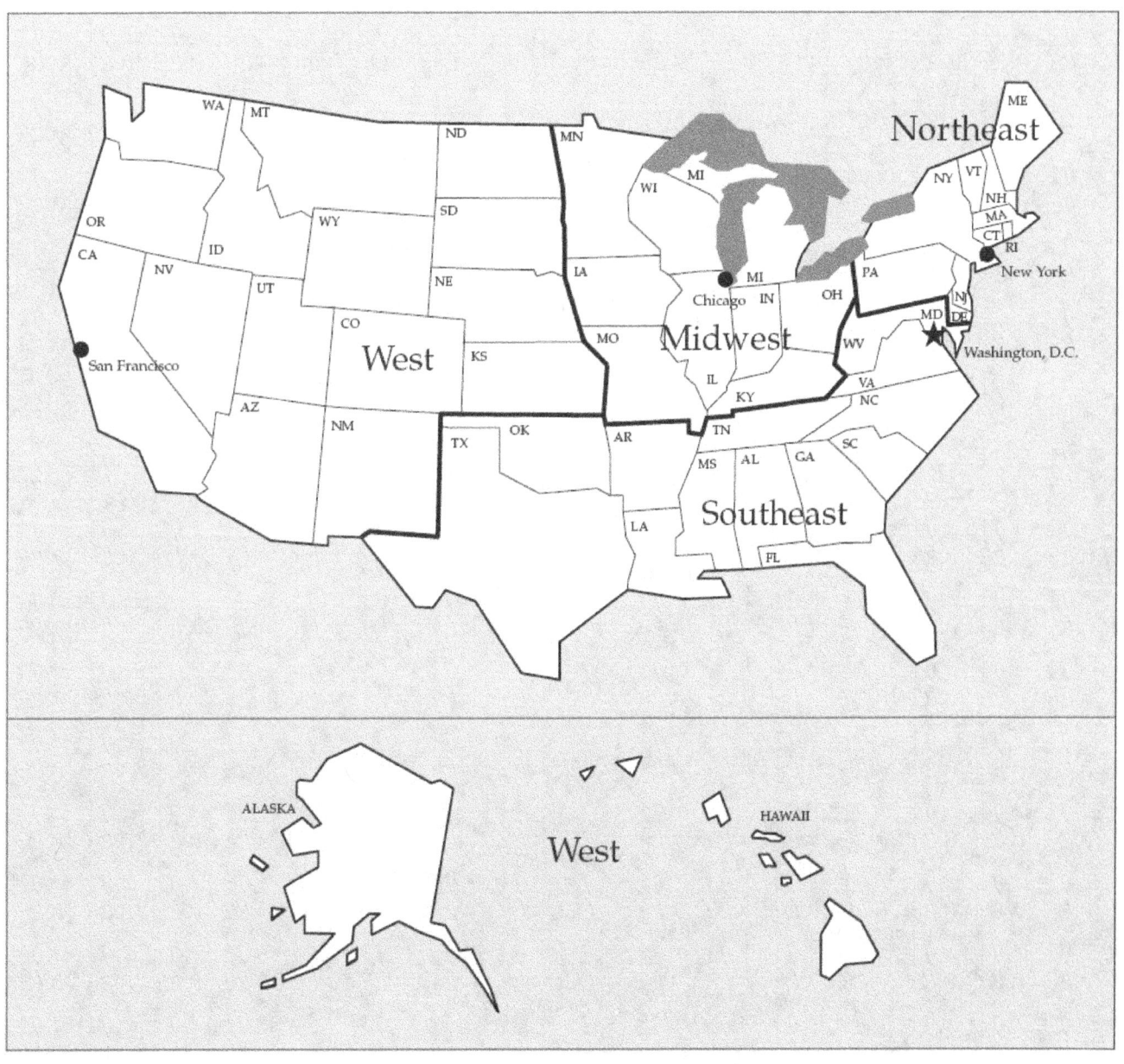

FEDERAL DEPOSIT INSURANCE CORPORATION REGIONS (SUPERVISION AND COMPLIANCE)

* Two area offices are located in Boston
(reports to New York) and Memphis
(reports to Dallas)

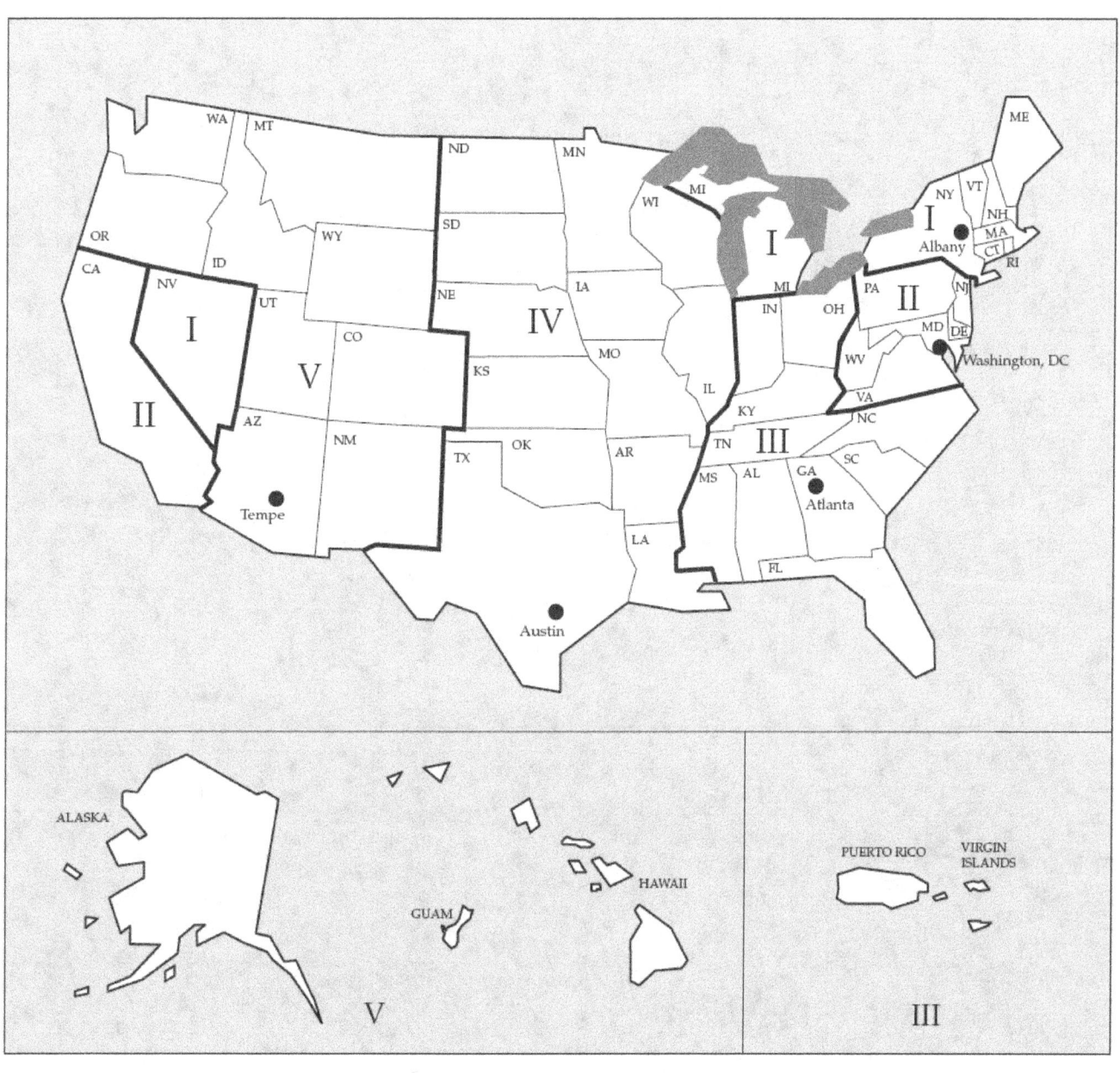

COMPTROLLER OF THE CURRENCY
DISTRICT ORGANIZATION

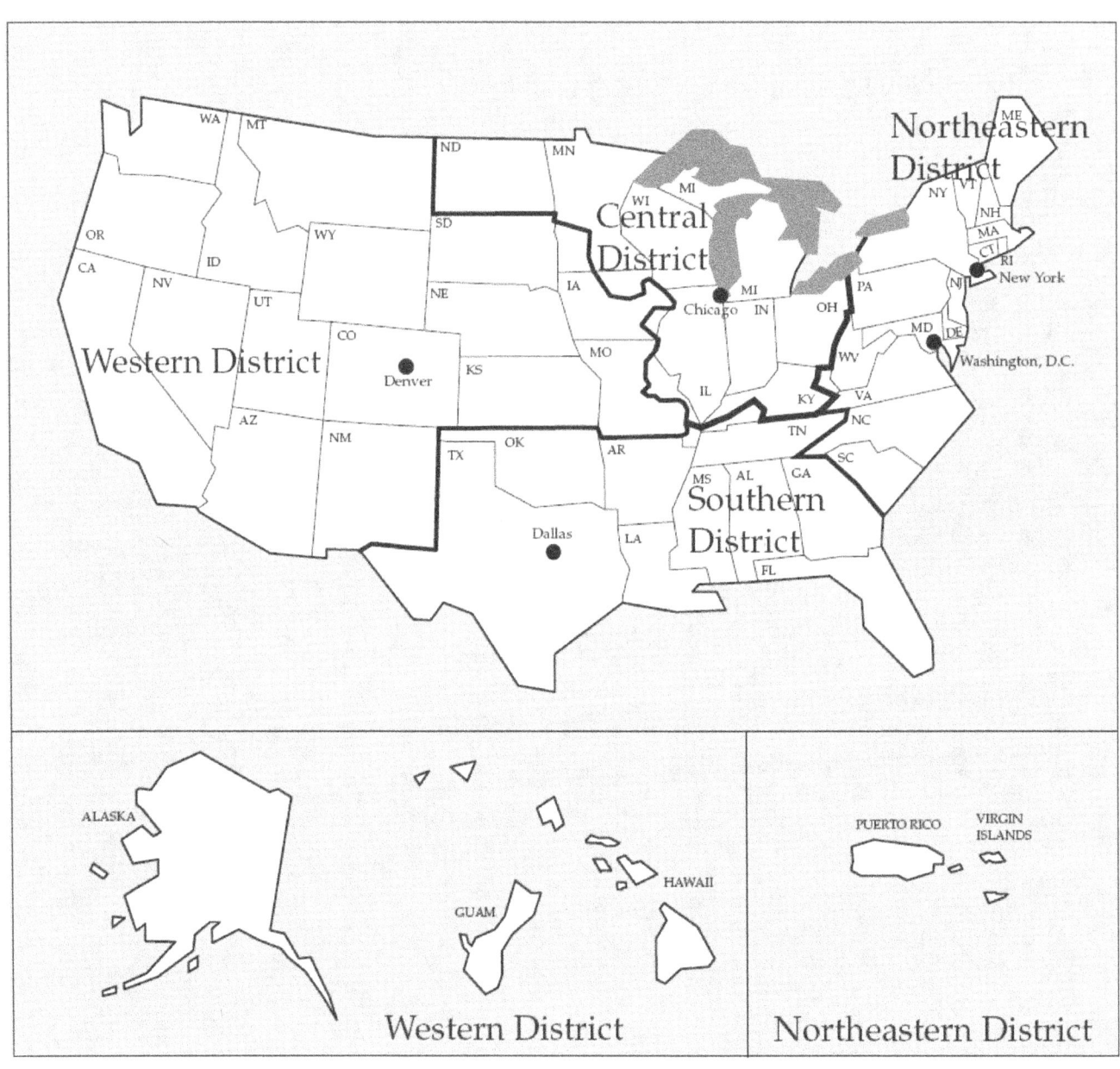

APPENDIX D: ORGANIZATIONAL LISTING OF PERSONNEL

Organization, December 31, 2011

Members of the Council

Debbie Matz, *Chairman*
  Chairman
  National Credit Union
    Administration (NCUA)

John Walsh, *Vice Chairman*
  Acting Comptroller of the
    Currency
  Office of the Comptroller of the
    Currency (OCC)

Daniel K. Tarullo
  Member
  Board of Governors of the
    Federal Reserve System (FRB)

Martin J. Gruenberg
  Acting Chairman
  Federal Deposit Insurance
    Corporation (FDIC)

Vacant
  Director
  Consumer Financial Protection
    Bureau (CFPB)

John Munn
  State Liaison Committee (SLC)
    Chairman
  Director
  Nebraska Department of
    Banking & Finance

State Liaison Committee (SLC)

John Munn, *Chairman*
  Director
  Nebraska Department of
    Banking & Finance

David Cotney
  Commissioner
  Massachusetts Division of Banks

Harold E. Feeney
  Commissioner
  Texas Credit Union Department

Douglas Foster
  Commissioner
  Texas Department of Savings
    and Mortgage Lending

Charles A. Vice
  Commissioner
  Kentucky Department of
    Financial Institutions

Council Staff Officer

Judith E. Dupre
  Executive Secretary

Interagency Staff Groups

Agency Liaison Group

Larry Fazio (NCUA)
John C. Lyons (OCC)
Arthur W. Lindo (FRB)
Sandra Thompson (FDIC)
Steven Antonakes (CFPB)
Michael Stevens (SLC Chair
  Representative)

Legal Advisory Group

Michael J. McKenna, *Chairman*
  (NCUA)
Julie L. Williams (OCC)
Scott Alvarez, (FRB)
Michael H. Krimminger (FDIC)
Leonard Kennedy (CFPB)
Margaret Liu (SLC Chair
  Representative (CSBS))

Task Force on Consumer Compliance

David Cotney, *Chairman* (SLC
  Chair Representative)
Grovetta N. Gardineer (OCC)
Carol Evans (FRB)
Luke H. Brown (FDIC)
April Breslaw (CFPB)
Moisette Green (NCUA)

Task Force on Examiner Education

Matthew J. Biliouris, *Chairman*
  (NCUA)
Shawn Clark (OCC)
Norbert Cieslack (FRB)
Philip D. Mento (FDIC)
Paul Sanford (CFPB)
Charlotte Nicholson (SLC Chair
  Representative)

Task Force on Information Sharing

Charles Lacek, *Chairman* (FDIC)
Jami Pictroski (CFPB)
Catherine Yao (NCUA)
Robin Stefan (OCC)
Michael Kraemer (FRB)
John Kolhoff (SLC Chair
  Representative)

Task Force on Reports

Robert F. Storch, *Chairman* (FDIC)
David Evans (CFPB)
Virginia L. Phillips (NCUA)
Kathy K. Murphy (OCC)
Arthur W. Lindo (FRB)
LeAnn M. Meyer (SLC Chair
  Representative)

Task Force on Supervision

John Lyons, *Chairman* (OCC)
Patrick M. Parkinson (FRB)
Sandra Thompson (FDIC)
Steven Antonakes (CFPB)
Matthew Biliouris (NCUA)
Charles A. Vice (SLC Chair
  Representative)

Task Force on Surveillance Systems

Robin Stefan, *Chairman* (OCC)
Matt Mattson (FRB)
Charles Collier (FDIC)
Andrew Trueblood (CFPB)
Lucinda V. Johnson (NCUA)
Bob Bacon (SLC Chair
  Representative)

Staff Members of the FFIEC

Shown are the FFIEC staff members at the Seidman Center in Arlington, Virginia, where they have their offices and classrooms for examiner education programs.

Retirement of Long-Term UBPR Coordinator

John Smullen, UBPR Coordinator for the Council retired in the second quarter of 2011 after 41 years of government service. After serving two decades with the OCC, John was a key member of the FFIEC Task Force on Surveillance Systems for the last 20 years. His expertise and dedication ensured the UBPR was both consistently maintained and regularly enhanced to serve the examination and surveillance needs of the federal and state banking agencies. Notably, John was instrumental in successfully moving UBPR processing to the CDR in 2010. His institutional knowledge was greatly valued.

Federal Financial Institution Examination Council staff members (from left to right): Ernie Larkins, Rosanna Piccirilli, Michelle Clark, Cathy Pritchard, David Vallee, Darlene Callis, Karen Smith, Judith Dupre, Jennifer Herring, Robert Basinger, Melanie Middleton, Juliet Pradier, and Cynthia Curry-Daniel.